KARATE

Date Due			
JAN 2 3 1992			
JAN 2 2 1992			
10.16.1 Feb 26/92			
FEB 2 1 1992			
FEB 1 2 1992			

About the authors

Dr. Daeshik Kim earned his B.A. degree at Georgia State University, his M.Ed. degree at Emory University and his Ed.D. at the University of Georgia. He has been involved in the martial arts since 1948 and now is a 7th degree black belt in judo (USJF), a 7th degree black belt in Tae Kwon Do, and has master's ratings in several other martial arts. Dr. Kim was the first person to introduce judo and karate into Georgia education. Dr. Kim is considered one of five pioneer masters in Tae Kwon Do in this country. Currently an assistant professor of Physical Education at the University of Texas at Austin, he has also taught at Georgia Southwestern College, Georgia State University, Emory University, the University of Georgia, City College of New York, and Yonsei University, Seoul, Korea. He is a former president of the National Collegiate Judo Association of the United States and was a director of the Korean Amateur Sports Association. Besides writing numerous articles for professional journals and magazines and coauthoring Judo in this series, Dr. Kim is the editor of Martial Arts Sports and the associate editor of Judo Times. Dr. Kim served as secretary of the Organizing Committee for the Third Tae Kwon Do World Championship in which 46 nations participated in Chicago in 1977.

Dr. Tom W. Leland is a psychotherapist in private practice in Honolulu, Hawaii. He received his M.D. from the Emory University School of Medicine in 1953, and after completing his internship and psychiatric residency on medical staffs in Washington, D. C. and Philadelphia, Pennsylvania, he served as a psychiatrist in the United States Navy.

Dr. Leland has been a student of the Oriental Martial Arts (judo, aikido and karate) since 1963, and has the rank of a 2nd degree black belt.

KARATE

Physical Education Activities Series

Daeshik Kim
7th Degree Black Belt
University of Texas
Austin

Tom W. Leland
2nd Degree Black Belt
Honolulu, Hawaii

SECOND EDITION

Wm C Brown Company Publishers
Dubuque, Iowa

Consulting Editor

Aileene Lockhart
Texas Woman's University

Evaluation Materials Editor

Jane A. Mott
Texas Woman's University

Printed in the United States of America   2-07079-02

Contents

Preface

This book is about the exciting, mysterious art and sport of karate (pronounced car-ah-tay). Karate is the most violent method of weaponless self-defense known to man. It has been called the ultimate in self-defense because it trains reflexes so keen that the practitioner can effectively defend himself from multiple assailants, even armed gang attacks. Yet pairs of karate students can spar vigorously together without protective equipment in complete safety. The art of karate is complex, sometimes tediously precise, and, of course, always potentially dangerous when safety rules are ignored; therefore, close supervision by a qualified instructor is required. This book is merely an introduction to the basic techniques of Japanese karate and Korean Tae Kwon Do. It is a guide and a supplement rather than, by itself, a teacher.

In this second edition, the authors have presented an expanded section on basic techniques as well as four Tae Kwon Do forms and a more detailed history and style variations of karate.

We live in an age of violence and aggression. Personal assault, muggings, and purse snatchings occur in public and in broad daylight. That unexpected once-in-a-lifetime emergency can happen. Hundreds of thousands of Americans, men and women, young and old, are studying this ancient and once-secret Oriental martial art as a life-saving, personal safety course. These students find karate and Tae Kwon Do more than just techniques of self-defense. In addition they are also safe fun-sports, healthful hobbies that can last a lifetime, and mentally stimulating challenges through which one can control inner anger. The highest goal of these martial arts is to teach inner peace and serenity so that anger and violence are no longer necessary. Karate masters believe that its ultimate aim lies not in victory or defeat, but in the perfection of character.

Community YMCAs, many colleges, and some high schools now offer karate courses, but students also study in private dojos or dojangs (exercise halls) in either group or private lessons. Karate has no season and can be practiced indoors or out without special equipment. Chapter 7 provides information about promotions through the ranks and suggestions for locating qualified instructors in your home community. Otherwise only the basic karate strikes, blocks, kicks, defensive and offensive techniques are described. The emphasis is on mastering basics. The important variations will be taught by the instructor.

Although the art of karate cannot be learned solely from books, supplemental reading is suggested. Rather than simply a "how to" book, special emphasis here is on the "why." Considerable space is devoted to karate's interesting philosophy, history, customs, and language. The Oriental philosophy of karate is centuries old, often misunderstood, and contains many intriguing paradoxes that have much appeal to the Westerner in today's world.

This book also contains a section on sparring techniques. Karate is a safe sport and learning no-contact sparring, without protective equipment, is possible once the basic techniques are mastered. Prearranged sparring of one and three-step fighting and free fighting for fun and in tournaments is described in this book. Some readers will want to go into sports competitions to test their newly learned skills against opponents of similar rank. Also included are a few karate forms or katas, mastery of which is required by some schools for promotions from white to yellow to blue belt. This introductory text gives the basic knowledge and essential techniques needed for promotion to the rank of brown belt (Japanese style) or maroon belt (Korean Tae Kwon Do style). In this revised edition there is an explanation of some of the differences between the various styles of karate, especially Japanese Karate and Korean Tae Kwon Do. Because of the recent television program, Kung Fu, and the many martial arts movies, the authors have added an introductory section on Chinese Kung Fu.

Objectives of the course in karate are: (1) To develop an appreciation for karate as an art and a sport; (2) To improve physical condition, mental discipline and emotional equanimity; (3) To develop a sense of responsibility for self and others; (4) To learn self-defense and personal safety.

Throughout this book you will find Evaluation Questions. The reader should attempt to answer these and should pose other suitable questions for himself. This is the way to learn. Keep check on your progress.

The authors hope that each reader will find the true meaning of nonviolence and nonaggression in the study of karate, though the journey may be a long and tedious one. Through karate, control of anger becomes a certainty and nonfighting, which is the ideal self-defense, becomes possible. The word karate means "empty hand." After many hours of practice the diligent student will discover that the empty karate hand turns away all weapons and violent blows. The art of the empty hand can be lifesaving.

The authors want to acknowledge the help of Mike Williams as editorial assistant. They also wish to express their thanks to Mike Billings for his professional photography. We are also very grateful for the special help of K.S. Shin, David Nemir, John Hasty, A. Helfman, and Joung Ok Suh.

Finally, the authors would like to express their thanks to those who helped with the first edition, without whose assistance this second edition would not have been possible.

The history of karate

1

THE HISTORY

Karate has a unique and unusual history. It was handed down centuries ago from Zen Master to Buddhist monk by word of mouth and always in strict secrecy. Even today everything done in karate can be traced back to some principle of Zen Buddhism. Although hundreds of pages, both legend and fact, have been written about karate's interesting origin, what is unknown would fill several libraries.

ANCIENT HISTORY: INDIA AND CHINA

In one sense, karate was born when primitive man first learned to wrestle and fight for his survival. Hieroglyphics from the Egyptian pyramids showed fighting techniques 6000 years ago that resemble karate of today. In the Eastern world, India had karate-like techniques as early as 3000 B.C. and Chinese Kempo boxing (chuan-fa) is thought to be 5000 years old. A primitive antecedent was the pancratium free-for-all fighting of the Greek Olympics. Although primitive boxing and wrestling were developed throughout the world and known to all races, karate, in its present form, is definitely Oriental. Its birthplace was both India and China, but primarily China. The Indian Buddhist priest Bodhidharma, known to the Japanese as Daruma Daishi, came to China in the sixth century A.D. and brought karate techniques and yoga meditation together as one in an effort to unite mind, spirit, and body. Bodhidharma taught meditation and Chinese Kempo, the direct forerunner of modern karate, at the Shaolin-ssu monastery. It was this religious connection with the ancient Shaolin style of Kempo that founded the Zen sect. For centuries the Shaolin Kempo was known only to the monks, but because marauding bandits plagued the countryside the secret techniques were taught for self-defense to neighboring farmers, and these spread throughout China. As China attacked, and sometimes allied with other nations, the Kempo techniques gradually spread throughout the entire Orient.

KOREAN TAE KWON DO

Since the late 1950s as more and more American soldiers returned from Korea, the Korean style of karate, Tae Kwon Do, has become very popular in the United States. A half dozen good textbooks already exist on this style, and in every large American city Korean instructors can be found to teach Tae Kwon Do.

Tae Kwon Do means "the way of fist and foot fighting" and is an ancient Korean martial art of weaponless self-defense.* Since its beginning, Tae Kwon Do has been the most effective method of unarmed self-defense known to man. It has been called the ultimate in self-defense because it trains the reflexes so keenly that the Tae Kwon Do practitioner can effectively defend himself against multiple assailants. Tae Kwon Do has recently been developed and modified into an injury-free competitive sport. Technically, Tae Kwon Do resembles a composite of boxing and French foot fighting, known as savate. Unlike judo and wrestling, Tae Kwon Do is not a body-contact sport. The punches, strikes, and kicks are pulled back before touching the sparring partner in practice sessions.

Many Americans incorrectly assume that Tae Kwon Do is simply a technique to forge the hands into a lethal weapon. Tae Kwon Do skills do not lead to savage or primitive behavior. On the other hand, television and motion pictures have made people think of Tae Kwon Do as just board- and brick-breaking. These techniques are but a small part of advanced Tae Kwon Do training. Tae Kwon Do training develops balance, speed, agility, strength, and rhythm. Coordination and great heart and lung capacity are also produced by Tae Kwon Do training. These are certainly desirable objectives of health, physical education and recreation programs in schools and communities.

Tae Kwon Do offers skills that may some day be life-saving, namely the skills of self-defense. Many people learn to swim and take courses in life-saving and water safety. Most parents encourage their children to take these courses, and everyone should enroll in them. Yet most of our lives are spent on dry ground. A life-saving course for survival on land is certainly worth consideration.

Tae Kwon Do is taught in graduated steps of basic and fundamental blocks, preparatory exercises, punches, strikes, kicks and conditioning. Form-training and cooling-off exercises are taught as well. Tae Kwon Do skills are as simple as swimming. However, instruction and practice are necessary if the student is to gain proficiency. Personal motivation and gratification are escalated as one learns the various aspects of this fascinating art.

*Literally *Tae* means to jump or kick or smash with the foot; *Kwon* means to punch or strike with the hand or fist. *Do* means "a philosophical way or way of life."

Achievement, satisfaction and contentment are tantamount to the development of a balanced, well-rounded mind. Active participation in Tae Kwon Do training can help one achieve these desirable qualities. Whether practiced as a sport or as an art, Tae Kwon Do enables one to visualize and then to obtain these goals.

Tae Kwon Do offers a physical and a mental challenge. Its values are superior to those of other combat sports. Tae Kwon Do can be described as a physical form of chess. One of the primary values of Tae Kwon Do training is its lessons in self-control and self-discipline. Tae Kwon Do training enables the student to channel his aggression in a positive and socially-accepted manner. The student learns that serenity improves performance and produces better results. Thus, Tae Kwon Do provides a setting for a feeling of emotional well-being, free from stress and fear.

The objectives of training are (1) to develop an appreciation for Tae Kwon Do as a sport and as an art; (2) to achieve physical fitness through positive participation; (3) to improve mental discipline and emotional equanimity; (4) to learn self-defense skills; and (5) to develop a sense of responsibility for one's self and others.

In Korea during the past two decades, elementary schools, colleges, and universities have introduced Tae Kwon Do into their physical fitness program. A number of schools, colleges, and universities in the United States have also introduced Tae Kwon Do. During the past decade more than 800 privately run Tae Kwon Do schools have come into existence in this country under about 1200 Korean instructors. In addition many YMCAs, community and/or recreation centers throughout the country are offering courses in Tae Kwon Do. The response to and the success of the clubs have been overwhelming. Now national, regional, state, and local Tae Kwon Do championships are held regularly and are extremely successful.

BRIEF HISTORY OF TAE KWON DO

The ancient Korean martial arts had their beginning hundreds of years before the birth of Christ, and in general included the use of many kinds of weapons. All forms of combat developed as a part of military training. The skills with various weapons became highly complex. Consequently Tae Kwon Do* developed as a branch of the martial arts limited to combat with the fists, hands, and feet.

The civilization of Korea is more than 4,307 years old, and has its own traditional culture and martial arts. The origin of Tae Kwon Do can be traced to the Koguryo, Paekje, and Silla Dynasties—the Three Kingdoms.

Archaeological findings such as the mural paintings on the royal tombs of the Koguryo dynasty, the stone sculptures of pagodas or temples produced in the Silla Dynasty, and documents written in the Paekje Dynasty contain many depictions of fighting stances, skills, and form movements very similar

*The way of fist and foot fighting.

to the present forms and skills of Tae Kwon Do. Therefore, it can be inferred that people in the Three Kingdoms engaged in exercises closely resembling Tae Kwon Do.

Spiritually, Korean culture and martial arts were strongly influenced and enriched by Hwa Rang Do, a military, educational, and social organization for noble youths that was instituted by King Jin Heung of the Silla dynasty. The Three Kingdoms were unified primarily by the spiritual influence of the Hwa Rang Do. Its codes of honor consisted basically of loyalty to the nation, respect and obedience to one's parents, honor and faithfulness to one's friends, courage and bravery of the battlefield, and avoidance of unnecessary violence and killings.

Many scattered descriptions of the Hwa Rang Do in written documents of the Three Kingdoms showed that the Hwa Rang Do not only regarded Tae Kwon Do as a part of physical and military training, but also recommended it as a recreational activity.

It was during the Koryo dynasty* (918-1392) that Tae Kwon Do attained its highest popularity. It was practiced by military officers and men and the general public as well as a martial art and recreational activity. It was also during the Koryo dynasty that Tae Kwon Do was technically organized and systemized by masters of those times. Military officers and masters were invited by the royal family to present demonstrations and to compete annually at the royal court.

Under King Taejo, founder of the Yi dynasty, Buddhism was supplanted by Confucianism as the state religion, thus providing major guidelines not only for official functions but also for the private lives of individuals. The ruling class of the dynasty strongly emphasized Chinese classical learning. As a result, civil officers gained higher esteem than military officers, socially as well as politically. Consequently the people became disinterested in martial arts, Tae Kwon Do declined in popularity, and its technical development was hindered.

Fortunately for the Korean martial arts, King Chongjo (1790) ordered Lee Duk Mu to write an official textbook on the military arts. That book, known as *Muye Dobo Tongji*, described and illustrated the Korean martial arts very clearly, and included a chapter on Tae Kwon Do.

Because physical activity was neglected, the decline of the martial arts continued in the latter half of the Yi dynasty, and the ruling class engaged in factional strifes and neglected national defense. As a result, Tae Kwon Do remained merely a recreational activity for ordinary people. No organized instruction was available, and Tae Kwon Do was handed down from father to son, or from teacher to disciple always in secrecy.

On August 22, 1910, the Yi dynasty was forcibly annexed to Japan. The Japanese colonial government not only banned cultural activities but also team sports and martial arts in order to destroy the Korean identity. In 1943, Japanese karate was introduced for the first time into Korea, and it gained in

*The English word *Korea* is derived from *Koryo*.

Can you draw a family tree for karate showing the relationships of the several martial arts?

popularity until Korea was liberated from Japan on August 15, 1945. Leaders in martial arts opened dojangs* (practice halls or schools for martial arts) under various names such as Kong Soo Do, Su Bak Do, Tang Soo Do, Kwon Bup and others. However, many leaders wanted to recover traditional Tae Kyon. The first conference for the unification of the dojangs and the search for the traditional art was held in July, 1946, but without success. Attempts to unify the different styles of the martial arts continued.

After much research and discussion, leaders of six major schools adopted the name Tae Kwon Do (the way of fist and foot fighting). In 1961, by governmental decree, a committee of seven members was organized to prepare for unification of schools, the Korea Tae Soo Do Association was given official membership in the Korea Amateur Sports Association (the national governing body for all sports in Korea). On August 5, 1965, the Korea Tae Soo Do Association was officially renamed the Korea Tae Kwon Do Association, and the word Tae Kwon Do was fully accepted by all Koreans.

On January 25, 1971, Mr. Un Yong Kim was elected president of the Korea Tae Kwon Do Association. Under his dynamic leadership the organization has significantly developed and advanced the discipline spiritually, physically, and technically, both within Korea and internationally. On November 30, 1972, the beautiful Kuk Ki Won building was erected. The Kuk Ki Won (literally the Institute for a National Sport) became the main educational and training center of the Korea Tae Kwon Do Association.

On December 1, 1972, the Korea Tae Kwon Do Association published Tae Kwon Do Kyo Bon, the complete textbook of Tae Kwon Do, containing twenty-seven new official forms.

On May 25, 1973, the First World Tae Kwon Do Championship was held at Kuk Ki Won with 200 champions from 17 nations participating under the auspices of the Korea Tae Kwon Do Association. Then, in 1974, the First Asian Tae Kwon Do Championship was successfully held at Kuk Ki Won.

The present membership of the Korea Tae Kwon Do Association numbers 1,500,000 and has 13 affiliated organizations in Korea—Korean Collegiate Tae Kwon Do Federation, Korean Secondary School Tae Kwon Do Federation, Korean Elementary School Tae Kwon Do Federation and its 10 provincial chapters.

Today, the Kuk Ki Won not only is the Headquarters for the World Tae Kwon Do, but also is the highest level educational institution for Tae Kwon Do training.

There are two other major Korean Karate organizations: Korean Soo Bak Do (Moo Duk Kwan, Tang Soo Do) under the leadership of Hwang Ki

*Literally translated, dojang means "way and place."

Fig. 1. Buddha found in ancient temples in pose similar to Tae Kwon Do stance.

and the International Tae Kwon Do Federation under the leadership of General Hi Hong Choi.

THE BIRTH OF MODERN KARATE: OKINAWA, JAPAN AND KOREA

The transformation of Chinese Kempo into modern karate took place in this century after an important intermediate stage on the Island of Okinawa. As early as A.D. 1100 Chinese Kempo was modified into Okinawan-te (te=hand) with special emphasis on open hand techniques. When the Japanese feudal lords conquered Okinawa in the seventeenth century and confiscated all weapons, the Okinawans continued to teach and use their te in secret. Once again, as had been true in the Shaolin-ssu monastery in A.D. 600, the techniques were taught in secret. In Japan, during the eighteenth and nineteenth centuries, the martial arts were refined by the fierce warrior class, the Samurai. These warriors made a life-time study of some twenty-five martial arts, including the use of the sword, spear, and bow and arrow. The technique of weaponless self-defense or jujitsu was only one of the Samurai's arts. In 1871 the Japanese shogun ended feudalism and decreed that swords could no longer be worn. The commoner had to learn bare-handed fighting lest he be murdered by maurauding bandits, and for a brief period of time until firearms were in general use, jujitsu was widely studied for its self-defense value. At the turn of the century, Professor Kano resurrected the dying art of jujitsu and transformed it into the popular sport of judo. Although ancient jujitsu included a number of kicking and punching techniques, modern judo uses only throws, pinning, choking, and bending and twisting joint locks.

In 1922 Ginochin Funakoshi demonstrated Okinawan-te to the Japanese.

The martial arts of jujitsu, judo, kendo and aikido were already becoming popular in Japan but there was no karate and Funakoshi was well received. Soon other Okinawan masters came to Japan to teach and the techniques were modified by the Japanese jujitsu students and the Korean students of Tae Kyon. The Japanese art adopted the new name karate, Kara for empty (also for Tang China) and te for hand. What we today call karate, then, is a fusion of Okinawan-te techniques modified by Japanese jujitsu.

Just before World War II karate was widespread in Japan and Korea, and, of course, te was and is still taught in Okinawa. China had developed Kung Fu and Tai Chi Chuan in addition to Kempo and in both Japan and Korea there were many different schools or styles of karate. Since World War II there have continued to be many different schools. In Japan today there are as many as seventy-five different styles. Only recently has free sparring (Kumite or Dae Ryon) been made relatively safe. For centuries the karate techniques were practiced alone in katas against imaginary attackers; since each strike was intended to be lethal, there was no way to test skills or practice with a fellow student. The only test was actual combat. In recent years training has emphasized pulling-back and controlling the kicks and punches so that it is safe to spar even without protective armor. Armor is, however, used in some contests today.

KARATE AND TAE KWON DO IN THE UNITED STATES

Very, very few Occidentals had even heard of karate until well after World War II. It was not until 1952 that America was introduced to karate by Master Masutatsu Oyama. Oyama traveled across the country with a professional wrestler, the Great Togo. Oyama's demonstrations of intricate karate forms or katas were often met with boos from the audiences. He began to demonstrate brick- and board-breaking techniques and then the American audiences applauded. In Japan and Korea the breaking techniques, used to test one's power, were a very small part of karate training, but brick breaking with the bare hands was something the American audience immediately appreciated. This exaggerated emphasis has only slowly changed in our country. Mr. Mas Oyama has returned to the United States several times since 1952 and he now has 100,000 students throughout the world. Most Americans now recognize that karate is a complex art and a sport as well as an effective technique of self-defense. Both Japanese karate and Korean Tae Kwon Do have become very popular in the United States since many American soldiers stationed in Korea and Japan were introduced to karate and Tae Kwon Do while overseas. It is estimated that there are now about 500,000 karate students in the United States studying Japanese, Korean, and Okinawan styles. Rising crime rates have increased interest in the practical self-defense aspects of the art. The spiritual emphasis, the Zen meditation and Yoga-like breathing exercises first introduced by Bodhidharma are all too often neglected by the American student. Since promotions to the higher ranks of black belt degree often require four to seven years for each promotion there are very few high ranking American teachers. Advanced students often prefer taking lessons from an Oriental teacher. Many excellent karate teachers have come to America, and good dojos or dojangs with 4th and 5th Dan black belt teachers are now available in every major city.

Interest in the martial arts, especially karate and Kung Fu has ballooned to fad-like popularity in the 1970s in America. Many older devotees complain that American karate today is too radically changed; that professional kick boxing and full-contact professional karate no longer resemble their sacred ancestors. While it cannot be argued that the U.S.A. has modified these ancient arts it is also true that the news and entertainment media have made karate and Kung Fu household words and as a result of the groundswell of interest fairly competent instruction is now available in every section of our country. Most recently movies and television dramas have stimulated a surge of new interest in the Chinese arts of Kung Fu and Tai-Chi Chuan. While karate and Tae Kwon Do are still the most popular, Kung Fu is gaining ground.

Very few Americans had ever heard of Tae Kwon Do before the late 1950's. Among the early pioneers and masters of Tae Kwon Do in America are Jhoon Rhee, Ki Whang Kim, Dae S. Kim, Henry Cho and Richard Chun as well as approximately twenty-five other master instructors. In October, 1974, the Amateur Athletic Union of the United States, Inc. (AAU) recognized Tae Kwon Do as an official sport, largely due to the efforts of Mr. Ken Min of the University of California at Berkeley. The 1st National AAU Tae Kwon Do Championship was held at Yale University in March, 1975. The 2nd Annual Tae Kwon Do Championship was held in Kansas City in March 1976. The 3rd Annual Tae Kwon Do Championship was held at the University of California at Berkeley in 1977. The AAU hosted the Third Tae Kwon Do World Championship of the World Tae Kwon Do Federation, in which more than 46 national teams, consisting of over 500 contestants, officials and master instructors, participated. This championship, held biennially, was held at the Chicago Amphitheater in September, 1977. This is the first official world Tae Kwon Do game to be held outside of Korea.

Kung Fu and Tai-Chi Chuan:

The term Kung Fu does not mean Chinese fighting as many assume but actually means patience with disciplines requiring time to master—and self-defense is only one of those disciplines. The birthplace of this fascinating art was also the Shaolin Monastery in China and originally encompassed four areas: wrestling, pugilism, weaponry, and health nourishment. Over thousands of years other disciplines were added including philosophy, scholarship, poetry, alchemy, and acupuncture. The core of the Kung Fu philosophy is in the teachings of I-Ching, Confucius, and Lao Tze. The list of skills to become a Sifu or Master were long and arduous. The martial art aspect was considered to be merely one of several stepping stones to enlightenment and serenity. Male and female Sifus called the self-defense aspect Kung Fu/wu shu (kuo-su or chung-kuo chuan). Traditionally Kung Fu resembles yoga rather than a martial art, although here in America we tend to think of Kung Fu as Chinese karate. There are many variations and styles of Kung Fu/wu shu (hereafter referred to simply as Kung Fu) but the two main sections are external and internal. The external is best described as hard, aggressive, and vigorous whereas the internal or soft variations emphasize pliability, relax-ation, and yielding. Many techniques are combinations of the "hard" and "soft" principles. Mountainous Northern China emphasized kicking (long fist) and Southern styles (paddy fields and boats) stressed hand (short fist) techniques. Throughout China today Kung Fu exercises are practiced daily by the masses as an intensive health program not only as a calisthenic but also for meditation, mental clarity and for unity of mind and body. Kung Fu students learn forms symbolizing the spirit of various animals including the styles of the dragon, tiger, leopard, snake and crane. After health exercise training the student usually begins with techniques in the use of the fist (chuan-shu) and legs (peishaolin) both soft and hard styles. Throwing tech-niques (swai-jow) are taught to intermediate students and the advanced learn weaponry techniques (pin-chie) including the art of the sword (chien-shu), spear (chiang-shu), curved sword (t'ao-fa) and staff or bo (kun-fa). There is much emphasis on "To-Na" breathing techniques and relaxation of the internal organs to free the energy known as Chi (called Ki in Japanese). At karate tournaments today one often sees Kung Fu stylists competing with students of karate and Tae Kwon Do. Excellent demonstrations of advanced kung fu forms and miraculous feats of strength and power are occasionally seen at National karate tournaments. Until this decade Kung Fu was taught only to Chinese students; now teachers, some poorly qualified, are available to occidentals everywhere.

Another popular Chinese martial art form is tai-chi chuan (nicknamed "tai-chi"). The words mean grand terminus pugilism, but the form resembles boxing hardly at all—except for very advanced forms. The movements are extremely slow, even to resembling a slow-motion ballet. The legs are rooted like a tree trunk and the arms seem to "float" and sway like the branches of a tree. Emphasis is on balance, being centered, and serene. Only advanced students learn push-hands and uprooting a partner's balance. There are many years of training before herbal medicine, acupuncture, and weaponry skills are taught. Unfortunately the fascinating philosophy is beyond the scope of this introductory text.

What karate is like

2

A visitor entering a karate dojo or dojang for the first time is likely to feel he has come into a strange new world. One is immediately struck with many paradoxes. Students in their white pajama-like costumes stand or kneel in silent meditation; they bow to the instructor and to each other and then what initially appeared to be some sort of a religious ceremony suddenly takes on the atmosphere of a silent barroom brawl. Students practice sparring in pairs, under the watchful eye of the ever present teacher; they seem determined to maim each other. The silent atmosphere is broken by blood-curdling shouts or kiais. Yet there is no injury and no one is angry or frightened. On a command from the teacher the apparent hostilities cease and the partners bow respectfully to one another. It is apparent to the shrewd observer that there is more going on here than practice fighting. Karate is a complex art, not unlike ballet; it is also a sport, not unlike boxing; and karate is a mental and moral exercise, indeed, almost a spiritual experience. In each practice session there is a concerted effort to unite mind, spirit, and body just as Bodhidharma sought to do with the Zen priests almost 2000 years ago.

Karate: for the Body Karate is a strenuous sport and art and instructors usually require that beginning students have a medical check-up before the first lesson. As with all active sports there is the laborious process of "getting-in-shape." Jogging daily, skipping rope and limbering-up, stretching calisthenics are prerequisites for learning. In each lesson, after meditation, ten to twenty minutes are devoted to warming, stretching, and limbering up the muscles. Special exercises are used to stretch the hamstring and calf muscles. Hand and foot toughening is done to some extent by all students but for board-breaking techniques special toughening exercises are needed—this should

Fig. 2.   Pose resembling upper block. Found in ancient Korean temples.

not be attempted without special instruction from the teacher. Reflexes must be quick. Since punches and kicks are delivered with the speed of sound, blocks must be almost at the speed of light. Balance is very important in all phases of karate and learning to relax between punches, kicks, and blocks is most difficult to learn for even athletically skilled students. Time and again the teacher will tell his students, novice and advanced alike, "relax-relax-then focus, then relax again." The karate forms (Kata or Hyong) require complete unity of mind and body, and the 180° turns and leaping kicks all require the exact amount of relaxation, balance, and sudden focusing of total body power into a single punch or kick. A special technique used to concentrate total body power into each punch is the Tae Kwon Do technique of the waist twist, which was developed by the Korean YMCA Tae Kwon Do Dojang. The waist twist allows relaxation until the last 9/10ths of the punch, then the waist, not hips, is twisted on a 45° to 90° rotation as the blow strikes its target, thus amplifying the punching power enormously. The strenuous physical exercises, including push-ups on the bare knuckles, are no more strenuous than other active sports and are easily mastered. The coordination, balance, and ability to relax between focuses of power are very difficult to master as they require complete control of body and mind—this is the physical challenge of karate. Remember the journey is itself the goal. There is no rush— practice daily and learn to relax.

   Karate: for the Mind   Obviously, karate requires intense concentration and an ability to focus one's attention intently for a moment, then turn the entire attention away to another direction and a new target. Mastering these new movements, some quite awkward, others only slightly different from ordinary movements, requires intelligence and patience. Each new technique

Have you planned a progressive conditioning program to supplement your Karate lessons? What forms of exercise have you chosen to improve strength, flexibility, and endurance?

may be something like rubbing the stomach and simultaneously patting the head while hopping on one foot—while relaxed. Karate is a physical game of chess and is not interesting to the dullard. All of this mental challenge and discipline is in itself worthwhile but karate offers still more—it is also a spiritual and a moral challenge.

Karate is Zen—so says Master Oyama and many other karate masters. Zen is a school of Buddhism that has been called the Religion of Immediate Reality. The aim of Zen is to awaken the student to his true self and thus bring about a high degree of self-knowledge through inward meditation. Zen students seek peace of mind through an enlightened awakening of an intuitive wisdom that they feel is dormant now in all people. Zen meditation tries to achieve "no mindedness," which may be acquired by concentration and special breathing exercises that are taught to advanced karate students. Karate when combined with Zen meditation can appreciably assist the student's quest for peace of mind and equanimity in the face of conflict and tension.

Fig. 3.   Meditation is a very important part of karate training.

Aggression is not merely a response to frustration, it is a deep-seated universal drive. The most crucial issue facing mankind today is whether or not man can learn to understand, ritualize, or otherwise control his aggression. This means sublimating his natural aggression into a ritual that is constructive, healthful, controlled, and yet effectively "lets off steam." Karate offers modern man such a discipline. Karate training allows the primitive aggression to explode and, simultaneously, allows the civilized man to carefully control the force and channel the energy—to withhold the violence until and only until he is physically attacked in such a way as to actually imperil his life. Karate, then, helps release some of the inner repressed rage of twentieth century man in a manner that is healthful, fun, mentally chal-

To what purposes can the study of karate be put? What are your own main reasons for engaging in this activity?

lenging and morally acceptable. This disciplined control is taught by the lifestyle of the karate teacher—the student learns this by trying to be like his teacher. It cannot be taught by word of mouth, only by the teacher's deeds.

In summary: Karate is for the mind, body and spirit.

Style Variations

There are many, many styles of Japanese, Korean, and Okinawan karate. To the novice their similarities far outweigh their apparently slight differences, but advanced students recognize the style differences at a glance. A general style difference (there are exceptions) is that hard and soft Okinawan styles emphasize hand movements with circular and open-hand techniques whereas most of the Japanese styles emphasize straight power punches and kicks. Korean Tae Kwon Do stresses kicks and jump kicking with emphasis on speed and balance. The traditional white gi also varies from school to school and now one often sees black, plaid, and multicolored gis at tournaments as well as silk Kung Fu uniforms with wide sashes. Although school loyalty quite naturally develops, all students are cautioned to not be openly critical or denigrating of other schools and styles. The wise student respects and quietly learns from other styles. It is appropriate to ask your teacher to comment on style preferences.

It is generally true that karate training in the Orient is much more strenuous and disciplined than training in the U.S.A. Oriental students traditionally pledge their very life to the sensei and are much less rank conscious than American students. In Japan and Korea the most arduous study takes place during the two hottest weeks of summer and the two coldest weeks of winter—outdoors. All school children study karate as a regular part of physical fitness class and several colleges devote their entire four year curriculum to the study of various martial arts.

OTHER MARTIAL ARTS: JUDO, AIKIDO AND HAPKIDO

Judo (pronounced joo-dough) means "gentle way." It is a two person artform based on ancient Japanese methods of bare-handed fighting. Judo is organized into a well-regulated, exciting, modern Olympic sport that somewhat resembles wrestling. Judo was founded in the late 1800s by Professor Jigoro Kano in his Tokyo school called the Kodokan. The forerunner of judo was jujitsu, which has a 1000 year old heritage quite similar to karate. Judo was known in the United States even before World War II and was in fact practiced by our robust president, Teddy Roosevelt. Judo is played on a mat

Fig. 4.   Meditation.

and strikes, punches, and kicks are not allowed. The sport is roughly divided into two main groups of techniques: Throws (from a standing position) and Grappling (while lying or sitting on the mat). A basic judo skill is learning the breakfall landing (ukemi). Before the new student can be safely thrown he must master the art of falling so that he can land safely, breaking his fall by slapping the mat with a shock-absorbing arm. Judo throws utilize the principle of giving-way to the opponent's strength. After pulling or pushing the partner off balance one then applies leverage and throws the partner to the mat using the hands, trips with the feet, twist over the hip, or one may deliberately fall first and while falling pull the off-balanced partner also to the mat. There are more than forty different throws that the student must master before being promoted to black belt. The grappling techniques include several pinning techniques, choking techniques, and arm locks. These are submission holds and the vanquished partner signals his defeat by tapping the mat twice.

Judo contests are won by one point (ippon), which is earned by a perfect throw or a combination of throw and a pinning, choking, or arm lock technique. The contest can be won by pinning the opponent for thirty seconds or a submission technique if there is a tap-out. The judo match lasts three minutes. Judo is a very well organized Olympic sport and the techniques are the same all over the world.

Aikido (pronounced aye-key-dough) means "way of spiritual harmony." It is the most modern of Japan's martial arts and its inventor Master Uyeshiba was actively teaching the art until his death at the age of 86 in 1970. Aikido is relatively unknown in this country, although demonstrations are occasionally seen at judo and karate contests. The Aikidoist wears a judo or karate costume (gi) with a swordsman's black skirt over his pants. Aikido is not a sport but a jujitsu-like style of "painless" self-defense. Aikido students use no kicking or striking but use come-along techniques, wrist twists, and turns and dodging techniques to subdue their opponent without causing any injury. The main school of Aikido emphasizes an unusual form of meditation called the "ki" in which the student learns to focus his power even though his muscles are relaxed. Aikido techniques (there are more than 2500 of them), are rather complex and often involve circular movements and turning around in circles. Aikido is gaining popularity in America but high ranking instructors are usually located only in large metropolitan areas. The skilled Aikidoist is very graceful to watch as he dodges and twirls away from five or six attackers at once. Master Uyeshiba developed a style of self-defense that achieves the ultimate in nonviolence and American students have dubbed Aikido, "The honorable art of getting the hell out of the way."

Hapkido (pronounced hop-key-dough) is a Korean art that combines karate and jujitsu—not to be confused with Japanese aikido. Thailand's kick boxing is becoming popular in the U.S.A. as is Japanese Kendo. Kendo (way of the sword) is a safe combat sport using a bamboo sword and complete body armor. Other weapons techniques (taught in some karate schools to advanced students) include the use of the bo (stick) the sai or jitte (three-pronged iron weapon) and nunchaku (2 pieces of wood joined by a cord or chain used as a striking, jabbing or poking club). Each of the weapon techniques have kata or forms. Kendo is "played" by pairs of opponents.

DOJO OR DOJANG MANNERS

Every student, regardless of rank or seniority, obeys an unwritten law upon entering any dojo or dojang. The manners, rituals, and customs of karate help set the tone of discipline and control. The student removes his shoes at the door of the dojo and bows ceremoniously on entering the practice area. At the beginning and at the end of each lesson the student bows to his teacher and he bows to his partners before and after each sparring practice. In the dojo, silence is mandatory and the students listen attentively to the teacher—no horseplay or loud talking is allowed. Boastfulness is very inappropriate and bullying behavior is strictly forbidden. Discipline is strict but always polite. The great respect for the teacher is more than a ritual, for the teacher has earned respect through his skill and manner. New students are always greatly impressed with the gentleness and humility of a senior karate teacher. Students all know that the teacher's opinion of their character, which includes good sportsmanship, humility, and gentleness, figures prominently in his decision about whether they are ready to learn advanced techniques. Physical readiness is not the only prerequisite for promotion.

Safety and Precautions   The attitude of all present in the dojo or dojang is one of great attentiveness, and for good reason—a misunderstood instruction or command could lead to serious injury. Each student quickly learns that the best safety precaution is wide-awake attentiveness. The senior students as well as the teacher all let the beginners know by word and deed that safety depends on playing the sport *exactly* by the rules. Karate is an injury-free sport *IF* the instructions of the teacher are followed carefully. Practic-

---

Most martial arts can be engaged in as competitive sports. Can you name and describe one that cannot?

---

ing advanced techniques, even if they look deceptively simple, without the teacher's supervision could easily lead to a broken bone.

Body armor and now gloves and foot padding are available for sparring or training.

KARATE COSTUME (GI, DO BOK)

The pajama-like karate costume is patterned after ancient Oriental clothing. The Japanese Karate gi or Korean Do Bok is a two-piece white cotton garment. The costume can be all black or white with belt colored trim. The colored belt denotes the wearer's official karate rank. The belt is worn over the jacket and is tied in front in a square knot. The gi or Do Bok should always be clean and in good repair. The feet and hands are bare. Do not wear rings or a wrist watch. An athletic supporter is usually worn and in free fighting practice the supporter should have a metal or plastic groin cup. Special padded armour is available but is not usually worn in most schools.

The karate uniform is considered the same as a holy robe and should not be over adorned. One school emblem and name may be suitable, but drawings, many different emblems, etc., are not considered to be in good taste.

Bowing   The Oriental bow is the customary way of showing respect, like the handshake or "hello" in the Western world. Like the handshake in boxing and football the karate bow announces, "I am ready," and at the end "Thank you." The karate bow is usually executed in the standing position but on ceremonious occasions may be performed from a kneeling position.

Fig. 5.   Standing Bow. Fig. 6.   Formal Kneeling Fig. 7.   Kneeling Bow.
                         Position.

In karate the action starts *immediately* after the bow, and the bow at the end of the match stops all further aggressive behavior.

TYPICAL KARATE CLASS

A well-planned karate lesson usually contains the following ingredients: Beginning Bow, meditation, calisthenics, practice basic skills (stances, strikes, blocks, and kicks), form practice and/or prearranged fighting practice. Free fighting practice is usually followed by an informal question and answer period. Then, new skills are introduced followed by closing meditation, warm-down exercises and closing bow. No horseplay or rough-house is permitted. The teacher is always accorded great respect and quiet attentiveness is mandatory.

SEASON, FACILITIES, EQUIPMENT

Karate can be practiced year-round indoors or outdoors. A hardwood floor is the best surface on which to practice, but mats or any other surface may be used. Advanced students may develop jumping kicks by jumping over ropes or chairs. In fall and spring it may be beneficial to work out outdoors, on the lawn or at the beach. For advanced students punching and kicking a heavy bag is also helpful.

Fundamentals of training

3

KARATE AND TAE KWON DO

The basic skills are very important in developing fundamental offensive and defensive maneuvers and kicking techniques. They are the ones that are considered most valuable by masters in the martial arts. Consequently, basic skills should be practiced over and over again until they have been thoroughly mastered. In either a competitive situation or a self-defense emergency one does not have time to stop and think before acting. He must rely on reflex actions, previously learned patterns that have become habitual through hundreds and thousands of repetitions of basic Tae Kwon Do—karate exercises. Elementary drills are thus the most important element in the art and sport of Tae Kwon Do.

One should practice these skills before a full-length mirror. You will need close personal supervision from a qualified instructor, but once your skills have been corrected, you can practice alone. Try to perfect your timing and your power focus. Remember that basic skills are the most effective and best skills.

All attacks can be practiced from any stance, and they should be practiced for use in all directions. Learning incorrect stances and movements will be a great liability later on.

Calisthenics Good physical fitness is very important. Jogging and rope jumping should be a matter of daily routine. Karate practice is strenuous and students can easily lose several pounds in sweat each lesson. Warm-up and warm-down exercises are most important. Consult your instructor for a calisthenic program for you. Karate students usually spend ten to twenty minutes of each class stretching and warming-up their muscles before practicing forms or free fighting. Sedentary students, especially middle-aged men, should be particularly careful about getting in shape with a *daily* exercise program before taking karate lessons. Place special emphasis on stretching the hamstring and waist muscles.

Balance and Footwork   Balance is a very important skill in karate. All advanced techniques are dependent on mastery of basic stances and maintaining good balance. In most body movements the center of gravity is low. Practice movement across the floor in front stance, then back stance and side stance. The feet slide over the floor in some movements and in others the feet are raised several inches as you turn or move. Try to develop your skills so that you move silently without "clunking" your feet down. As you move, your balance should be stable. When turning or moving diagonally do not cross legs. Beginners find it difficult to move without bobbing up and down. Try to keep the head level and moving in a straight line. Practice in front of a mirror and have your instructor check your progress. Again, learning incorrect stances will be a great liability later on. Initially practice movements with feet only; later hand movements, for example, straight punches or blocks, are added. Much practice is required in these early lessons. When basic skills are mastered, then complex turns and jump kicks are easily added.

Breath Control   Most people, when punching, throwing or even hitting a golf ball, hold their breath. Karate students learn to exhale forcibly when striking or blocking because this gives extra power. The karate yell, Kiai or Kihap, is believed to impart even an extra power beyond that of silent exhalation. For one thing, the occult shout certainly startles or at least distracts the opponent and at the same time it seems to give the student an extra spurt of confidence. You can demonstrate this for yourself when in later training you begin to practice board breaking. Karate students are encouraged to practice nasal rather than mouth breathing. Advanced students will learn yoga-like Zen breathing techniques that will facilitate their ability to focus power and be less distractable.

VITAL POINTS

There are certain areas on the human body that are especially vulnerable. These invisible points or areas are called vital points because a sharp blow or rap to one of these points could be lethal. The testicles, the solar plexus ("breadbasket"), the throat, and the bridge of the nose are commonly known spots of great tenderness. A fist strike to the shoulder, a forearm or thigh may be very painful but hardly lethal. However, a fist strike with the same force to the temple, heart or over the liver (right lower rib cage), spleen (left lower rib cage), or kidneys could cause great damage and could easily cause a fatal hemorrhage. The vital points depicted in these diagrams are "winning points" in a karate contest. Most of the vital points are in the midline of the body at junction points, that is, the neck, waist, groin, knee, and ankle.

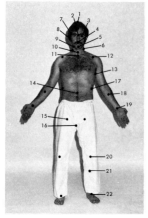 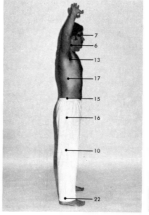 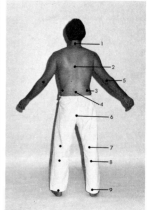

Fig. 8. Vital Points. (front view)

Fig. 9. Vital Points. (side view)

Fig. 10. Vital Points. (back view)

Front

Vital Points	Blows Delivered by
1. Skull	(Bottom of the fist. Knife hand)
2. Bridge of Nose	(Forefist, Back of the fist, Knife hand)
3. Eye	(Finger spear hand)
4. Philtrum	(Fist, Palm heel, Foot edge)
5. Chin	(Fist, Palm heel, Ball of the foot)
6. Side of Neck	(Ridge hand, Knife hand, Ball of the foot)
7. Temple	(Fist, Hand, Palm heel, Ball of the foot)
8. Ear	(Hand, Bottom of the fist)
9. Jaw	(Fist, Palm heel, Ball of the foot, Foot edge)
10. Adam's Apple	(Knuckle fist, Knife hand, Spear hand)
11. Windpipe	(Knuckle fist, Finger spear hand)
12. Clavicle	(Bottom-fist, Knife hand)
13. Armpit	(Knuckle fist, Elbow, Ball of the foot)
14. Solar Plexus	(Fist, spear hand, palm heel, Ball of the foot, Foot edge, knee)
15. Abdomen	(Fist, Ball of the Foot, Foot edge, Heel, Knee)
16. Groin	(Fist, Hand, Ball of the foot, Foot edge, Instep, Knee)
17. Rib	(Fist, Backhand, Knife hand, Ball of the foot, Heel, Foot edge, Instep, Knee)

Think about the concept of control in karate. Can you explain the various forms of control that have a bearing on performance and meaning of this art?

18.	Inner Forearm	(Fist, Knife hand)
19.	Inner Wrist	(Fist, Knife hand)
20.	Side Knee	(Foot edge)
21.	Shin	(Ball of the foot, Foot edge, Heel)
22.	Instep	(Foot edge, Heel)

Back

	Vital Points	Blows Delivered by
1.	Base of Cerebellum	(Knuckle fist, Knife hand, Ball of the foot)
2.	Upper Back	(Fist, Palm heel, Elbow, Ball of the foot)
3.	Kidney	(Fist, Palm heel, Elbow, Ball of the foot, Foot edge, Heel, Knee)
4.	Small of the Back	(Fist, Palm heel, Ball of the foot, Heel, Knee)
5.	Inside and outside Elbow	(Bottom of the fist, Back of the hand, Knife hand, Palm heel, Ball of the foot)
6.	Coccyx	(Ball of the foot, Foot edge, Heel, Knee)
7.	Hollow of the Knee	(Ball of the foot, Foot edge, Heel)
8.	Side of Knee	(Foot edge)
9.	Achilles Tendon	(Ball of the foot, Foot edge, Heel)

WEAPONS

Basically any part of the human body can be used as karate weapons; however the hands, elbows, feet, knees and forehead are the weapons of choice in karate. The striking surfaces of these weapons are shown here:

The Karate Fist

The first two knuckles (never the 3rd and 4th) are the striking surface.* The karate fist is very tight and mimics the principle of "brass knuckles." The trimmed fingernails and fingertips bite into the palm and the thumb tucks

*James H. Larose and Daeshik Kim, "Knuckle Fracture," *Journal of the American Medical Association*, vol. 21, no. 4, October 21, 1968, pp. 95-98.

  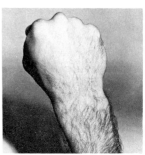

Fig. 11. Fore-Fist
(front view)

Fig. 12. side view.

Fig. 13. top view.

down the 1st and 2nd fingers. The fist is hard and tight and is basically the most common weapon in karate. The wrist is never bent up or down; in fact a book placed across the wrist shows no gaps and is well-balanced.

The Karate Knife Hand (Fig. 14)

The very little bean-sized pisiform bone at the wrist on the little finger side is the striking surface. The open hand is called a knife hand and is tense and the small striking surface is aimed at the target. The fingers are absolutely tight together.

Spear Hand (Fig. 15)

Fingers are extended tightly, with thumb slightly bent upward. Spear hand is used in thrust to face, neck, solar plexus.

The Karate Foot (Ball)

Knife Foot Edge (Fig. 16)   The outside edge of the foot is called a knife foot or foot edge.

Fig. 14. Knife Hand.

Fig. 15. Spear hand.

 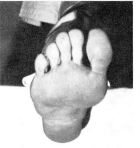 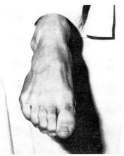

Fig. 16.   Knife foot.   Fig. 17.   Ball of the foot. Fig. 18.   Instep.

Ball of Foot (Fig. 17)   Used in kicks to the face, abdomen and front vital points.

Instep (Fig. 18) Basically used in kicks to the groin, side of face and ribs.

Knee (Fig. 19)

Used in kicks to the face, abdomen, and groin, and is known as knee kick. Useful for short distance sparring or as a practical self-defense in a close situation.

Heel (Fig. 20)   Used in kicks to abdomen, face and stamping the opponent's instep or body.

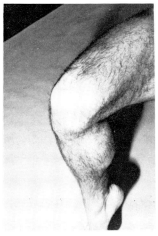 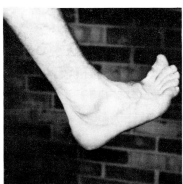

Fig. 19.   Knee.   Fig. 20.   Heel.

Elbow   Used in forward motion to attack chin or solar plexus; rear motion to attack solar plexus; in a side forward or rear motion to attack the side of face or ribs.

What are the four most commonly used stances and have you practiced them until you can move instantly from one to another without hesitation?

Stances

The stances constitute the obvious first step in Tae Kwon Do training. In order to execute offensive and defensive techniques with maximum power, the student must have perfect balance and must maneuver from a perfect Tae Kwon Do stance.

There are many stances, but those that are most commonly used by students, from beginner to black-belt, are the following: horseback, front, back, and ready. In short, mastering the science of karate is founded on stances.

1. **Attention Stance** (Open toe stance) (fig. 21). The heels are together, the toes pointing outward at a forty-five-degree angle to one another.
2. **Closed Toe Stance** (fig. 22). The feet are parallel and the toes are pointed straight ahead. The ankles are touching one another.
3. **Ready Stance** (fig. 23). From a heels-together stance, move one foot aside so that your feet are spread twelve inches apart with the toes pointed outward at a forty-five-degree angle to one another.
4. **Horseback Stance** (fig. 24). Spread your feet thirty to forty inches apart, and bend your knees so that your hips are about six inches lower than usual. Your center of gravity should be located halfway between your feet.
5. **Front Stance** (fig. 25). Move your right foot forward and bend your right knee. The distance between the toe of your left foot and the toe of your right foot should be about thirty inches (drop to knee of rear leg and measure two fists to heel of front foot) and sixty to seventy percent of your weight should be on your right foot. Your left knee should be locked.
6. **Back Stance** (fig. 26). Move your right foot a step forward so that the distance between your right heel and the inside edge of your left foot is eighteen to twenty inches. The right and left feet should be placed at a ninety-degree angle to one another and sixty to seventy percent of the weight should be placed on your left foot. This stance is the left back stance (left foot forward is right back stance).
7. **Crane Stance** (fig. 27). Bend one knee slightly and place the other foot to the side or back of the knee (position of foot depends on the karate style practiced).
8. **Tiger Stance** (Cat Stance) (fig. 28). Right foot straight forward with the left foot placed at a forty-five-degree angle. Only the ball of the right foot is touching the floor and the heel of the right foot is raised two to three inches. Both knees are pointed inward and your center of gravity should be placed on the left foot (vice versa for the right tiger stance).
9. **Crossed Foot Stance** (Hooked Stance) (fig. 29). Cross your feet, one behind the other and at the same time bend your knees.
10. **Pigeon Toe Stance** (fig. 30). Spread feet about the width of the shoulders, toes are pointed in, heels are pointed out. Knees of both feet are slightly pointed inward.

Fig. 21. Attention Stance (open toe)

Fig. 22. Closed Toe Stance.

Fig. 23. Ready Stance.

Fig. 24. Horseback Stance.

Fig. 25. Front Stance.

Fig. 26. Back Stance.

Fig. 27. Crane Stance.

Fig. 28. Tiger Stance.

Fig. 29. Crossed Foot Stance.

Fig. 30. Pigeon Toe Stance.

Basic offensive and defensive skills

4

The basic skills in this chapter are very important in developing fundamental offensive maneuvers, defensive maneuvers, and kicking techniques. Students should realize these basic skills and maneuvers are the best techniques, and they should be practiced over and over again until they are thoroughly mastered. In a real situation or in competition, a person does not have time to stop and think; he must rely on reflex actions previously learned by repeating basic skills. Ground work is the most important consideration!

Fifteen defensive techniques, fifteen offensive techniques, and fifteen kicks will be presented in this book. These techniques may be used in combination.

I. Basic Defensive Skills
   A. Blocks—Fist or Knife Hand
      1. **Rising Block** (Face Block) (fig. 31). This block should be made with the outside of the forearm, which is at a slight angle with the rest of the arm. The arm is two fists distance from the head. The palm should be turned away from the head.
      2. **Body Blocks** (inside-outside, outside-inside) (fig. 32).
         a. Inside-Outside—The block should come from in front of the opposite hip (right hand, left hip and vice versa), up and across in front of the body. It should stop with the elbow bent 120° and the fist on the same level as the shoulder. The palm of the hand is facing toward you and the block is made with the outside of the forearm.
         b. Outside-Inside—Raise your fist above your ear and snap arm around in front of you, stopping with the fist on the same

Fig. 31. Rising Block.   Fig. 32. Body Blocks.   Fig. 33. Low Block.

level as your shoulder and the elbow bent 120 degrees. Your palm should be toward you. Body blocks can be practiced from either back stance or front stance.

3. **Low Block** (fig. 33). Your blocking hand is brought up over the opposite shoulder and moves down and across the front of the body, stopping two fists distance above the knee. The block is made with the outside of the forearm.

4. **Double Middle Block** (Augmented Block) (fig. 34). This is the same as an inside-outside middle block with the addition of the little finger of the other hand touching the elbow of the blocking hand for support. The supporting hand's palm is up. This block can be practiced from either back stance or front stance.

5. **Upper X Block** (fig. 35). This block is made with knife hands crossing at the wrists and palms facing to the sides. The block is two fists above the forehead.

6. **Lower X Block** (fig. 36). This block is made with fists crossed at the wrists and held in front of the groin.

7. **Double Side Block (High)** (fig. 37). Swing both arms out to the side of your head with your palms facing inward. The elbows should be at an angle greater than ninety degrees and the fists slightly higher than the head.

8. **Double Side Block (Low)** (fig. 38). Swing the arms down with palms facing down. The fists should be two fists higher than the knee.

9. **Single Side Block** (with horseback stance) (fig. 39). From a horseback stance bring your hands across your body, block to the side with your right hand, bringing your left hand to rest at your hip. The blocking hand should be made with either the fist or knife hand.

Fig. 34. Double Middle Block.

Fig. 35.   Upper X Block.

Fig. 36.   Lower X Block.

Fig. 37. Double Side Block (High).

Fig. 38. Double Side Block (Low).

Fig. 39. Single Side Block.

10. **Knife Hand Face Block** (fig. 40). This block is performed from the back stance. The right arm is bent at a 120-degree angle and the first joint of the index finger is held at eye level. The left hand is held in a knife hand, the forearm parallel to the floor and the elbow held out from the body. The wrist should be placed in front of the solar plexus.

11. **Knife Hand Body Block** (fig. 41). This block is the same as the knife hand face block except that the first joint of the index finger is held at shoulder level.

12. **Knife Hand Low Block** (fig. 42). In this block move your right foot forward into a left back stance and execute a lower knife

Fig. 40.   Knife Hand Face Block.

Fig. 41.   Knife Hand Body Block.

Fig. 42.   Knife Hand Low Block.

Fig. 43.   Low Augmented Block.

Fig. 44.   Wedge Block (Palm Up)

Fig. 45.   Wedge Block (Palm Down)

hand block bringing the first joint of your index finger a little lower than the belt. It will not be close to your forward leg.

13. **Low Augmented Block** (fig. 43). This is the same as a lower block except that the opposite fist is placed near the elbow of the blocking arm in order to reinforce the block.

14. **Wedge Block** (palm up) (fig. 44). Cross both wrists in front of your chest. Bring both forearms out simultaneously, blocking with the inside of the forearm. Fists should be shoulder level. Fists are pointed upward.

15. **Wedge Block** (palm down) (fig. 45). In this block the blocking surface is the outside of the forearms. Palms are pointed downward.

II. Basic Offensive Skills
   A. Fist Punch (variation middle knuckle).
      1. **High Punch** (fig. 46). The fist should strike at eye level.
      2. **Middle Punch** (fig. 47). The fist should strike the solar plexus.
      3. **Low Punch** (fig. 48). The fist should strike the groin.
      4. **Double Punches** (fig. 49). Punch with both fists at the same time. The arms are parallel and the fists should strike the solar plexus.
      5. **Double Side Strikes** (fig. 50). Bring fists over your head with the third joints of the index fingers nearly touching. Bring both fists down in a semicircle striking with the bottom of the fist. Double side strikes and double straight punches can be used in combination.
      6. **U-Punches** (fig. 51). Hold one fist on your hip and the other one directly above it. (Palms face each other.) The fist on your hip should strike at the eye level. The other fist should strike the groin. The punches are delivered simultaneously.
      7. **Side Punch** (fig. 52). Deliver this punch from a side stance. The arm and fist should be in a straight line with the shoulder.
   B. Spear Hand and Eye Poke
      1. **Two Finger Eye Poke** (fig. 53). Poke your attacker's eyes with your middle and index fingers.
      2. **One Finger Eye Poke** (fig. 54). Poke one of your attacker's eyes with your index finger.
      3. **Spear Hand** (fig. 55). Hold all your fingers close together and point them straight out. Lock your thumb back close on your hand. Strike the abdomen or solar plexus with the spear hand.
   C. Knife Hand
      1. **Outside to Inside** (fig. 56). Raise your hand, level with your head so the fingers touch just (palm faces ear) behind the ear. Your elbow should be raised also. Strike quickly snapping your hand

Fig. 46.   High Punch.   Fig. 47.   Middle Punch.   Fig. 48.   Low Punch.

What is the point of aim for each of the following punches: low punch, middle punch, double punch, high punch, side punch, U punch?

Fig. 49. Double Punch. Fig. 50. Double Side Strikes. Fig. 51. U-punches.

Fig. 52. Side Punch. Fig. 53. Two Finger Eye Poke. Fig. 54. One Finger Eye Poke.

around so you strike your opponent on his neck. The palm of the hand is facing up.

2. **Inside to Outside** (fig. 57). Raise your hand over your opposite shoulder (right hand over left shoulder and vice-versa) so the fingers touch behind the ear (palm faces ear). Snap your arm out

Fig. 55. Spear Hand. Fig. 56. Outside to Inside Knife Hand Strike. Fig. 57. Inside to Outside Knife Hand Strike.

Fig. 58. Front Elbow Strike. Fig. 59. Rear Elbow Strike. Fig. 60. Front Side Elbow Strike. Fig. 61. Rear Side Elbow Strike.

quickly to strike your opponent's neck. The palm of the hand is facing down.

3. **5-Way Hand Chops.** Execute an outside to inside chop; an inside to outside chop; an outside to inside chop striking at a 45-degree angle with a line perpendicular to the opponent's neck; and bring the last chop straight down.

4. **Reverse Knife Hand Chop.** Bend your thumb under the palm of your hand. Strike with the area around the joint where the thumb connects to the hand. Swing your arm back and around to strike.

5. **Elbow Strikes** (4 way). (1) Bring the elbow straight up as if to hit someone on the chin (fig. 58). (2) Swing the elbow straight back as if hitting an attacker from the rear in the abdomen (fig. 59).

(3) Swing your elbow to the left in front of you as if striking an attacker in the mouth (fig. 60). (4) Swing your elbow back to the right as if striking an attacker in the mouth (fig. 61).

D. Additional Hand Techniques

1. **Palm-Heel Strike.** Hold the hand with fingers up at a ninety-degree angle with the arm. Strike with the area of the hand below the thumb.
2. **Open Palm.** Strike with the flat of the hand with an open palm.
3. **Back Hand.** Hold the fingers and thumb straight out. Strike with the area around the back of the hand.
4. **Hammer Fist.** Make a regular fist. Strike with the side of the hand like a knife hand chop.
5. **Reverse Hammer Fist.** Strike with the area formed by closing the thumb around the first finger.
6. **Back Hand Punch.** Strike with the first two knuckles but do not turn the fist around as in a regular punch.

III. Kicks

A. Front Kicks

1. **Front Snap.** Raise your knee to the same level as your hips. Snap the foot out with the toes pointed up so you kick with the ball of your foot.

   a. Low—Kick the groin. (fig. 62A)
   b. Middle—Kick the abdomen or solar plexus. (fig. 62B)
   c. High—Kick the face. (fig. 62C)

Fig. 62A. Front Snap (Low) Fig. 62B. Front Snap (Middle) Fig. 62C. Front Snap (High)

2. **Front Instep Kick** (fig. 63). Kick your leg straight out to about the height of your hips. Your toes should be pointed straight out. This kick is to the groin.

3. **Front Thrust Kick** (fig. 64). Bring your knee straight up then thrust your leg straight out in front of you. Your toes should be pointed up. This kick is aimed at the stomach or solar plexus and used to stop a lunging attacker.

B. Side Kicks

1. **Side Snap Kick** (fig. 65). Raise the instep of one foot to the knee of the opposite leg (knee is pointed out). Swing the leg straight out to the side in a snapping motion and back again. You should kick with the outside edge of your foot.

Fig. 63. Front Instep Kick. Fig. 64. Front Thrust Kick.   Fig. 65. Side Snap Kick.

2. **Side Thrust** (figs. 66A and 66B). Raise the instep of one foot to the knee of the opposite leg. (The knee of the raised foot is straight up.) Twist your hips and thrust the leg straight out to the side, kicking with the outside edge of the foot. The kick should be aimed at an opponent's head.

3. **Slap Kick** (Inside to Outside) (figs. 67A and 67B). Keeping the kicking leg straight, raise it in a large circular motion in a clockwise direction. This technique is used to kick the opponent's jaw, temple or jaw with your instep, knife foot edge or the side of the heel.

4. **Slap Kick** (Outside to Inside) (figs. 68A and 68B). This kick is the reverse of the inside-outside slap kick, the circular motion is in a counter clockwise direction.

C. Back Kicks

1. **Back Kick** (fig. 69). Raise your knee straight up with toes pointed down. Kick straight behind you striking with the heel of your foot. Look over the shoulder on the same side you are kicking. The kick should go as high as possible.

Fig. 66A.
Side Thrust
Kick.

Fig. 66B. Side
Thrust Kick.

Fig. 67A. (Inside
Outside) A.

Fig. 67B. Slap Kick
(Inside Outside) B.

Fig. 68A. Slap Kick
(Outside inside) A.

Fig. 68B. (Outside inside)
B.

Fig. 69. Back Kick.

2. **Back Swing Kick** (fig. 70). Keep the leg you kick with straight and stiff. Swing it straight up from the floor aiming it toward an opponent's head. You should kick with the back of your heel.

D. Various Kicks

1. **Heel Kick** (fig. 71). Raise your knee up then thrust it down striking with the heel of your foot. Your toes should be pointed up. This kick is used for striking feet or someone on the ground.

2. **Round House Kick** (figs. 72A, 72B, and 72C). Raise your leg with

Fig. 70. Back Swing Kick.   Fig. 71. Heel Kick.

Fig. 72A. Roundhouse Kick-A (Side View).   Fig. 72B. Roundhouse Kick-B.   Fig. 72C. Roundhouse Kick-C Executed.

the knee bent out to your side. Snap the leg around straight out in front of you kicking with the ball of your foot. Twist your hips into it as you snap your leg around.

3. **Sacrifice Kick** (fig. 73). There are many variations to this kick. One is to drop to the rear knee (falling to the rear), bring up both hands to the side of the face and bring them to the floor to support your upper body as it comes down. Execute a side kick or a round house kick.

4. **Double Front Kick** (figs. 74A and 74B). Assume either front or back stance, one foot kicks either the knee or the groin. Before this foot touches the ground kick either the face or solar plexus with the other foot.

5. **Side Jump Kick.** Jump high to your side in the direction of your target. Execute a side kick in the air, chambering both legs just prior to impact.

Can you name the kicks that involve a sideward movement of the leg? How many have you mastered on the left side? On the right side?

Fig. 73.   Sacrifice   Kick.

Fig. 74A.   Double Front Kick-A.

Fig. 74B.   Double Front Kick-B.

6. **Knee Kick** (fig. 75). Knee is used to strike either the groin or the face. When the knee is raised the toes should point downward, toward the floor.
7. **Advanced Jump Kicks.** These kicks use kicks already described but are executed while in the air. You usually jump high with the leg you are going to kick with then kick. Examples of jump kicks are: double front snap, flying round house, flying side, flying spinning, back kick.

Fig. 75.   Knee Kick.

Forms and sparring

5

The karate form (Kata or Poom Se in Korean) is the embodiment of precision drill. About forty percent of the student's time is spent mastering the forms.

In ancient karate, form practice was the only way to learn techniques since only an imaginary opponent could withstand the lethal blows. All masters still feel that form practice is absolutely essential to understanding karate.

There are more than one hundred forms in existence in Japan and Korea, but very few students master more than a dozen forms in a lifetime study of the art. Most schools require perfection of about ten forms for promotion to Black Belt. The forms must be performed perfectly. They require skillful balance, controlled breathing, strength, speed, and endurance. Each new form is a mental challenge and requires intense concentration.

The forms are combinations of blocks, kicks, and strikes defending against attack from several different directions. Each new form must be practiced several hundred times before it is perfected. The esthetic qualities of a well-executed form are breathtaking to watch.

In this introductory book only five forms are presented; namely, Pal Gye Il Chang (Pal Gye #1), Pal Gye Yi Chang (Pal Gye #2), Pal Gye Sam Chang (Pal Gye #3), of the Korean Tae Kwon Do Association and the World Tae Kwon Do Federation; Chon ji of International Tae Kwon Do Federation, and Naifanchi of Japanese karate. Pal Gye Il Chang is a fairly simple pattern to learn and many white belt beginners are introduced to forms with this pattern. The Naifanchi #1 kata or form is a sample from a popular Japanese style of karate. It is often introduced at the brown belt rank, but mastery seldom is achieved until the Dan or black belt rank.

In practicing these forms use a full length mirror to perfect each movement. After complete memorization of the form try to perfect the timing and power focusing. You will need close personal supervision by a qualified teacher but once your movements have been corrected you can practice alone, with gradually increased power and in complete safety. Try not to bob up and down. Move slowly until your teacher tells you to speed up. In advanced study focus the eyes and try to imagine real opponents attacking you from several different directions. In the Orient, form practice is considered to be equal in importance to free fighting practice.

Forms are logical and predetermined combinations of stances, blocks, punches, strikes and kicks against imaginary attackers converging from all directions. As a physical education and fitness activity, form training is considered equal to free sparring. By participating in form training, students improve their fitness and, ideally, perfect all basic stances, skills, movements, and strategies.

Form training requires concentration and an ability to focus one's attention intently for a moment then turn the entire attention away to another direction and a new target. Form training requires complete unity of mind and body. The 180 degree turns and leaping kicks require total balance, strength, speed, agility, coordination, relaxation, breath control, and ability to suddenly focus all of one's power in a single punch or blow.

Karate or Tae Kwon Do exercises, especially form training, can be practiced safely and effectively at any time, anywhere, without equipment or facilities, individually, or with a group. Therefore it is an ideal physical fitness activity for all.

In summary: Karate or Tae Kwon Do form training promotes self-defense and physical fitness.

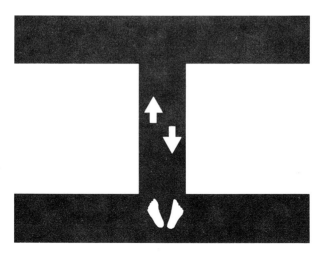

NOTE: Line of performance is:
The performer should be facing 12 o'clock high (A).

What is a karate form? Of the more than 100 forms in existence approximately how many must be mastered for promotion to Black Belt? How many forms might you expect to master in a lifetime of study of karate?

This form includes twenty steps performed as if the student were defending himself against several assailants.

An overview of the entire form will make it easier to understand the sequence of steps. The student is to imagine that he is standing on the face of a clock, and also on a letter "H" lying on its side. Advances will be explained in terms of the "H," and turns in terms of right, left, clockwise, counterclockwise, and the figures on the clockface.

REMEMBER: The importance of the ceremonial bow at the beginning and the end of the Poom-Se cannot be overemphasized.

Before you practice, take note of the fact that in most movements it is essential to keep your center of gravity low. Practice moving across the floor in front stance, and then in back stance and in side stance. In some movements the feet slide over the floor, and in others the feet are raised several inches during a turn or some other move. Also, practice movements must be silent and firm, without any stamping of the feet. Be careful to keep your balance stable as you move. Beginners find it difficult to move without bobbing up and down. Try to keep your head level and moving in a straight line.

PAL GYE IL CHANG

• *Assume the attention posture* [*facing 12 o'clock*].

• *Bow.*

• *Assume a ready stance.*

1. Pivot counterclockwise on your right foot to 9 o'clock, and into a left-front stance. Simultaneously, execute a left low block.
2. Step forward into a right stance, and simultaneously execute a right outside-inside body block.
3. Pivot clockwise on your left foot, passing 12 o'clock to 3 o'clock and going into a right front stance. Simultaneously, execute a right low block.
4. Step forward into a left front stance, and simultaneously execute an outside-inside left body block.
5. Pivot counterclockwise on your right foot to 12 o'clock, and into a left front stance. Simultaneously, execute a left low block.
6. Step forward into a left back stance, and simultaneously execute a right inside-outside body block.
7. Step forward into a right back stance and simultaneously execute a left inside-outside body block.
8. Step forward into a right front stance, and simultaneously execute a right body punch, yelling.
9. Pivot counterclockwise on your right foot, passing 6 o'clock to 3 o'clock and going into a right back stance. Simultaneously, execute a left knife hand block.

10. Step forward into a left back stance, and simultaneously execute a right inside-outside body block.
11. Pivot clockwise on your left foot, passing 6 o'clock to 9 o'clock, and going into a left back stance. Simultaneously, execute a right knife hand block.
12. Step forward into a right back stance, and simultaneously execute a left inside-outside body block.
13. Pivot counterclockwise on your right foot to 6 o'clock and into a left front stance. Simultaneously, execute a left low block.
14. Move forward into a right front stance, and simultaneously, execute a right outside-inside knife hand strike. Your palm is up and aimed at your opponent's neck.
15. Move forward into a left front stance, and simultaneously execute a left knife hand strike.
16. Move forward into a right front stance, and simultaneously execute a right body punch, yelling.
17. Pivot counterclockwise on your right foot, passing 12 o'clock to 9 o'clock and going into a left front stance. Simultaneously, execute a left low block.
18. Step forward into a right front stance, and simultaneously execute a right body block (the same movement as in #2).
19. Pivot clockwise on your left foot, passing 12 o'clock to 3 o'clock and going into a right front stance. Simultaneously, execute a right low block (the same movement as in #3).
20. Step forward into a left front stance, and simultaneously execute a left body block (the same movement as in #4).

- *Pivot on your right foot, and resume the ready stance.*
- *Assume attention posture.*
- *Bow.*

PAL GYE IL CHANG

Attention   Bow

IL CHANG

Ready Stance 1   2   3   4   5

6   7   8   9   10   11

12   13 (Side View) 14 (Side View)   15 (Side View)16 (Side View)   17

18   19   20   Ready Stance   Attention   Bow

PAL GYE YI CHANG

NOTE: The line of performance is the same as the first form.

- *Assume the attention posture [facing 12 o'clock].*
- *Bow.*
- *Assume a ready stance.*

1. Pivot counterclockwise on your right foot to 9 o'clock, and into a left front stance. Simultaneously, execute a left face block (rising block).
2. Execute a right front kick. Step down and assume a right front stance and simultaneously execute a right body punch.
3. Pivot clockwise on your left foot, passing 12 o'clock to 3 o'clock and going into a right front stance. Simultaneously, execute a right face block.
4. Execute a left front kick. Then plant your foot in a left front stance and simultaneously execute a left body punch.
5. Pivot counterclockwise on your right foot to 12 o'clock and into a right back stance. Simultaneously, execute a low left knife hand block.
6. Step forward into a left back stance, and simultaneously execute a right knife hand block (middle knife hand block).
7. Step forward into a left front stance, and simultaneously execute a left face block.
8. Step forward into a right front stance, and simultaneously execute a right body punch, yelling.
9. Pivot counterclockwise on the right foot, passing 6 o'clock to 3 o'clock and going into a left front stance. Simultaneously, execute a left face block.
10. Execute a right front kick. Plant your foot in a right front stance, and execute a right body punch simultaneously.
11. Pivot clockwise on your left foot, passing 6 o'clock to 9 o'clock and into a right front stance. Simultaneously, execute a right face block.
12. Execute a left front kick. Plant your foot in a left front stance, and simultaneously execute a left body punch.
13. Pivot counterclockwise on your right foot to 6 o'clock and into a right back stance. Simultaneously, execute a left low augmented block (Guh Deul A Mak Gi).
14. Step forward into a left back stance, and simultaneously execute a right middle augmented block. Execute it from inside to outside.
15. Step forward into a right back stance, and simultaneously execute a left body block. Execute it from outside to inside.
16. Step forward into a right front stance, and simultaneously execute a right body punch, yelling.
17. Pivot counterclockwise on your right foot, passing 12 o'clock to 9 o'clock and into a left front stance. Simultaneously, execute a left face block.
18. Execute a right front kick. Then plant your foot in a right front stance, and simultaneously execute a right body punch (the same movement as in #2-2).
19. Pivot clockwise on your left foot, passing 12 o'clock to 3 o'clock into a right front stance. Simultaneously, execute a right face block (the same movement as in #3).
20. Execute a left front kick. Then plant your foot in a left front stance, and simultaneously execute a left body punch (the same movement as in #4).

- *Pivot on right foot and resume ready stance.*
- *Assume attention stance.*
- *Bow.*

PAL GYE YI CHANG

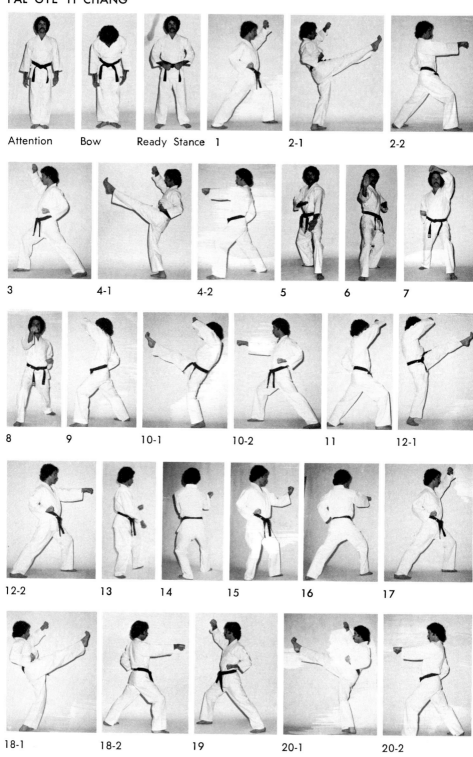

Attention   Bow   Ready Stance 1   2-1   2-2

3   4-1   4-2   5   6   7

8   9   10-1   10-2   11   12-1

12-2   13   14   15   16   17

18-1   18-2   19   20-1   20-2

PAL GYE SAM CHANG

NOTE: The line of performance is the same as first form.

- *Assume the attention posture [facing 12 o'clock].*
- *Bow.*
- *Assume a ready stance.*

1. Pivot counterclockwise on your right foot to 9 o'clock and into a left front stance, and simultaneously execute a left low block (A Rae Mak Gi).
2. Step forward into a right front stance, and simultaneously execute a right body punch.
3. Pivot clockwise on your left foot, passing 12 o'clock to 3 o'clock into a right front stance. Simultaneously, execute a right low block.
4. Step forward into a left front stance, and simultaneously execute a left body punch.
5. Pivot counterclockwise on your right foot to 12 o'clock and into a left front stance. Simultaneously, execute a left low block.
6. Step forward into a right front stance, and simultaneously execute a right face block (rising block).
7. Step forward into a left front stance, and simultaneously execute a left face block.
8. Step forward into a right front stance, and simultaneously execute a right face punch, yelling.
9. Pivot counterclockwise on your right foot, passing 6 o'clock to 3 o'clock into a right back stance. Simultaneously, execute a left knife hand block (middle knife hand block).
10. Step forward into a left back stance, and simultaneously execute a right knife hand block (middle knife hand block).
11. Pivot clockwise on your left foot, passing 6 o'clock to 9 o'clock into the left back stance, and simultaneously execute a right knife hand block.
12. Step forward into a right back stance, and simultaneously execute a left knife hand block.
13. Pivot counterclockwise on your right foot to 6 o'clock and into a right back stance. Simultaneously, execute a left body block, from inside to outside.
14. Pivoting on both your feet, turn to face 12 o'clock, and shift your weight to a left back stance. Simultaneously, execute a right body block, from inside to outside.
15. Step backward into a right back stance, and simultaneously execute a left body block from outside to inside, facing 12 o'clock.
16. Step backward into a left back stance, and simultaneously execute a right body block from outside to inside, facing 12 o'clock.
17. Step backward into a right back stance, and simultaneously execute a left body block from outside to inside, facing 12 o'clock.
18. Pivoting on both your feet, turn to face 6 o'clock, shift to a left back stance, and simultaneously execute a right body block from inside to outside, facing 6 o'clock.
19. Pivot counterclockwise on your right foot to 9 o'clock and into a left front stance. Simultaneously, execute a left face block.
20. Step forward front into a right stance, and simultaneously execute a right face punch.
21. Pivot clockwise on your left foot, passing 12 o'clock to 3 o'clock and into a right front stance. Simultaneously, execute a right face block.
22. Step forward into a left front stance, and simultaneously execute a left face punch, yelling.

- *Pivot on the right foot, and resume the ready stance.*
- *Assume the attention posture.*
- *Bow.*

PAL GYE SAM CHANG

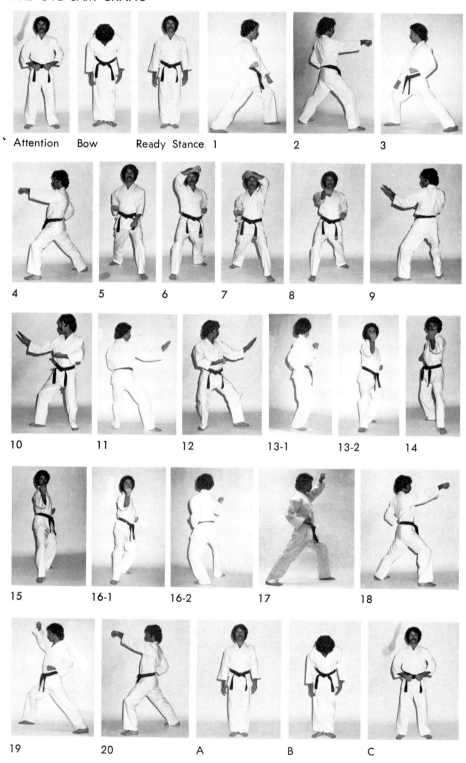

Attention   Bow   Ready Stance   1   2   3

4   5   6   7   8   9

10   11   12   13-1   13-2   14

15   16-1   16-2   17   18

19   20   A   B   C

CHONJI (Means heaven and earth).

NOTE: Line of performance is:
The performer should be facing
12 o'clock high (A).

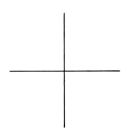

1. Attention facing 12 o'clock.
2. Bow and attention stance (no picture).
3. Ready stance.
4. Face 9 o'clock, move into left forward stance and execute left lower block.
5. Step forward into right forward stance and execute right middle punch.
6. Pivot on left foot passing 12 o'clock to three o'clock into right forward stance and execute right lower block.
7. Step forward into left forward stance with left middle punch.
8. Move left foot toward 12 o'clock into left forward stance and execute left lower block.
9. Step forward into right forward stance and execute right middle punch stop.
10. Pivot on left foot 180° passing 3 o'clock to 6 into right forward stance and execute right lower block.
11. Step forward into left forward stance with left middle punch.
12. Move left foot to 3 o'clock forming right back stance and make left inside-outside middle block.
13. Step forward into right forward stance with right middle punch.
14. Pivot on left foot 180° passing 6 o'clock to 9 forming left back stance and making right inside-outside middle block.
15. Move into left forward stance facing 9 and execute left middle punch.
16. Turn to 6 o'clock forming right back stance with left inside-outside middle block.
17. Step to 6 o'clock into right forward stance and execute right middle punch.
18. Pivot on left foot 180° passing 9 o'clock to 12 o'clock forming left back stance and make right inside-outside middle block.
19. Move into left forward stance with left middle punch to 12 o'clock.
20. Move into right forward stance with right middle punch.
21. Move right foot back to form left forward stance and execute left middle punch.
22. Move left foot back into right forward stance with right middle punch (yell).
23. Bring left foot up to ready stance.
24. Bring left foot to right foot at attention.
25. Bow.

CHONJI

NAIFANCHI (Known as Iron Horse #1).

NOTE: Line of performance is:
The performer should be facing
12 o'clock high (A).

1. Bow.
2. Ready stance (closed toes; left palm over back of right hand).
3. Look to 3 o'clock, cross left foot over right foot (slightly bend knees).
4. Stamping kick with right foot into horse riding stance with horizontal knife hand strike to 3 o'clock (left fist drawn to hip—side of the body).
5. Strike right palm with left elbow in direction of 3 o'clock.
6. Pull right fist to hip with left fist over right fist.
7. Look quickly toward 9 o'clock and execute left lower block (6-7 done quickly).
8. Execute right turning punch to 9 o'clock bringing left fist to hip.
9. Step toward 9 o'clock by crossing right foot over left (keep hands in same position).
10. Bring right foot down into horseback riding back riding stance with stamping motion and simultaneous back fist strike to face in direction of 12 o'clock.
11. Make lower block with right forearm and upper block with left forearm while still in riding stance facing 12 o'clock.
12. Strike with left back fist toward 12 o'clock bringing right fist underneath left arm near elbow (10-12 done quickly).
13. Look toward 9 o'clock, bring right foot to left knee and lower it immediately into riding stance with left outside-inside middle block to 9 o'clock.
14. Look toward 3 o'clock, bring right foot to left knee and lower it immediately into riding stance with left outside-inside middle block to 3 o'clock.
15. Pull right fist to hip with left fist directly over it and palms facing.
16. (A) Execute horizontal middle punch to 9 o'clock with both hands (yell). (B) Bring left hand under right arm for knife hand strike, to the left.
17. Strike with left knife hand to 9 o'clock bringing right fist to hip (No. 17-29 movements are the same movements as No. 5-16, only toward the left).
18. Strike left palm with right elbow toward 9 o'clock.
19. Bring left fist to hip with right fist directly over it.
20. Look toward 3 o'clock and make a lower block with right forearm to 3 (19-20 done quickly).
21. Make a left turning punch to 3 o'clock while bringing right fist to hip.
22. Looking to 3 o'clock and keeping hands in same position, cross left foot over right forming right X stance (hooked stance).
23. Bring right foot down into riding stance with stamping kick and a simultaneous left back fist strike to 12 o'clock.
24. Facing 12 o'clock in riding stance, make left lower block and right upper block simultaneously.
25. Strike with right back fist to face in direction of 12 o'clock bringing left fist under right arm near elbow.
26. Look toward 3 o'clock, bring right foot to left knee and lower it immediately back into riding stance with right inside-outside middle block to 3 o'clock.
27. Look toward 9 o'clock, bring left foot to right knee and lower it immediately back into riding stance with right outside-inside middle block to 9 o'clock.
28. Bring left fist to hip with right fist directly over it and palm facing.
29. Execute horizontal punch to 3 o'clock (yell).
30. Bring right foot to left foot forming closed toes ready stance with left palm over back of right hand.
31. Attention.
32. Bow.

The names of Tae Kwon Do and karate forms are listed for readers' information:

I. KOREAN FORMS

(A) Official forms of the Korean Tae Kwon Do Association and the World Tae Kwon Do Federation.

Name of Form (Poom Se)	Requirement for Rank
(1) Pal Gye #1 (Il Chang)	8th Keub (Class) or (Gup)
(2) Pal Gye #2 (Yi Chang)	7th Keub
(3) Pal Gye #3 (Sam Chang)	6th Keub
(4) Pal Gye #4 (Sa Chang)	5th Keub
(5) Pal Gye #5 (Oh Chang)	4th Keub
(6) Pal Gye #6 (Yook Chang)	3rd Keub
(7) Pal Gye #7 (Chil Chang)	2nd Keub
(8) Pal Gye #8 (Pal Chang)	1st Keub
(9) Koryo	1st Dan Black Belt (Degree)
(10) Kum Gang	2nd Dan Black Belt
(11) Tae Back	3rd Dan Black Belt
(12) Pyung Won	4th Dan Black Belt
(13) Sip Jin	5th Dan Black Belt
(14) Ji-tae	5th Dan Black Belt
(15) Chung Kwon	6th Dan Black Belt
(16) Silla Hansoo	6th Dan Black Belt
(17) Il Yeo	7th Dan Black Belt

For junior division (under 16 years old) are Tae-geuk forms. Tae-geuk forms are primarily for elementary and junior high school boys and girls.

(B) Official forms of the International Tae Kwon Do Association.

(1) Chon Ji	10th Keub (Class)
(2) Tan Gun	9th Keub
(3) To San	8th and 7th Keubs
(4) Won Hyo	6th Keub
(5) Yul Kok	5th Keub
(6) Chung Gun	4th Keub
(7) Toi Gye	3rd Keub
(8) Hwa Rang	2nd Keub
(9) Chung Mu	1st Keub
(10) Kwang Gye	1st Dan Black Belt
(11) Po Un	2nd Dan Black Belt
(12) Kae Back	3rd Dan Black Belt
(13) Yu Shin	4th Dan Black Belt
(14) Chung Jang	5th Dan Black Belt
(15) Ul Ji	5th Dan Black Belt
(16) Sam Il	6th Dan Black Belt
(17) Choi Young	6th Dan Black Belt
(18) Ko Dang	7th Dan Black Belt

(19) Se Jong   7th Dan Black Belt
(20) Tong Il   8th Dan Black Belt
(21) Moon Moo   8th Dan Black Belt

(C) Other forms which were known in Korea (listed at random).
     (1) Ki Bon Hyong #1, #2, #3 (known as Basic forms)
     (2) Pyong Ahn Cho Dan (#1)
     (3) Pyong Ahn Yi Dan (#2)
     (4) Pyong Ahn Sam Dan (#3)
     (5) Pyong Ahn Sa Dan (#4)
     (6) Pyong Ahn Oh Dan (#5)
     (7) Chul Ki Cho Dan (Known as Nai Fan Chi, Nae Bo Jin or Ki Ma) #1
     (8) Chul Ki Yi Dan (#2)
     (9) Chul Ki Sam Dan (#3)
     (10) Ba-Sai (Bal Sack)
     (11) Sip Soo
     (12) Yun Moo
     (13) Kong Sang Goon (Kwan Kong)
     (14) Ro Hai
     (15) Ban Wol
     (16) Jin Do
     (17) Ahm Hak
     (18) Ja Eun
     (19) So Lim Chang Kwon
     (20) Dan Do Hyong (Dagger Form)

II. JAPANESE FORMS

More than fifty-five karate forms exist in Japan, however some well-practiced Japanese forms are listed at random.
(1) Ki Hon Kata #1, #2, #3
(2) Tai Kyo Ku #1, #2, #3
(3) Pin An Sho Dan (Pinan #1)
(4) Pin An Ni Dan (#2)
(5) Pin An San Dan (#3)
(6) Pin An Yo Dan (#4)
(7) Pin An Go Dan (#5)
(8) Nai Han Chi Sho Dan (Known as Tek Ki Sho Dan #1)
(9) Nai Han Chi Ni Dan (#2)
(10) Nai Han Chi San Dan (#3)
(11) Nai Han Chi-Koshiki Kata (Ancient form)
(12) Basai Dai
(13) Basai Sho
(14) Rou Hai
(15) Jinto
(16) Ji Te
(17) Ji On

(18) Ni Sei Shi
(19) Sen Se Ru
(20) Kyokushinkan Kata
(21) Yantsu
(22) Tensho
(23) Sanchin
(24) Saiha
(25) Tsushibo
(26) Kanku
(27) Seienchin
(28) Hangetsu

SPARRING

The beginner is not introduced to free sparring until he has begun to understand basic offensive and defensive techniques, has begun practicing the forms, and has been introduced to prearranged fighting and semi-free fighting.

Prearranged fighting consists of a pattern of blows, blocks and counterattacks that are determined in advance so that both fighters know exactly which techniques are to be used. This allows the beginner to practice slowly at first and develop speed when the techniques have been learned. Chances of injury are minimized because both participants know what to expect in advance. One person is assigned the role of defender while the other is the attacker. The defender stands in the ready stance while the attacker stands in the front stance and has executed a lower block. The attacker advances and executes a punch. The defender blocks and executes a counterattack. Prearranged fighting is classified as one, two or three step fighting. This designation depends on whether the attacker advances one, two or three steps before the defender launches a counterattack.

Semifree fighting expands the concept of prearranged fighting in that a series of kicks and punches are used in any sequence the fighter desires. A specified number of attacks are used, then the roles of attacker and defender are reversed. Semi-free fighting contains elements of both prearranged fighting and free sparring. As the student becomes more advanced the techniques should become more complex.

Free fighting is more spontaneous than either prearranged fighting or semi-free fighting. Both participants are free to attack at will and may counterattack at any point that they feel they have an opportunity to score. The roles of attacker and defender are not static and shift back and forth constantly. While in general any technique may be employed in free sparring, there are certain proscribed techniques such as attacks to the eyes, genitals, and knees because failure to exercise sufficient control in attacking these areas could result in serious injuries.

Free fighting is the simulation of combat. Techniques are focused very close to the opponent's body without making contact unless protective equipment is used. It is important that the student not attempt free-fighting until his instructor decides that he is ready and to do so only under his instructor's supervision. Otherwise serious injuries may result.

Physical fitness is important. Being in good condition lessens the possibility of injury and gives one the stamina to execute the technique he has learned. Knowing what to do makes little difference when you are too exhausted to complete the technique.

Be confident. Don't be unsure of yourself. If you are, your opponent will sense it and use your hesitation to his advantage. If you are afraid or tired, just remember that your opponent is just as afraid and just as tired as you are. The contest is just as demanding for him as it is for you.

Good training not only builds endurance but it also allows you to execute the techniques you have learned smoothly and crisply.

Use strategy. Don't repeat the same attack and counterattack moves to the point that your opponent knows exactly what to expect from you and can set you up for whatever techniques he chooses. Do the unexpected. Change stances often. Since each stance has its peculiar strengths and weaknesses, your opponent will be confused and will not know what to expect. Avoid your opponent's strengths and seek his weaknesses. Make him fight your kind of fight. Tire him out.

Use all of the techniques you have learned. Make your stances well defined. Don't just kick and swing your arms. Be concerned with good form.

Be relaxed. Tension inhibits effective sparring because it slows responses and is more likely to be telegraphed (indicated in advance as pulling back the fist before striking) since movement from a tense position is easy to detect. It is easier for most people to avoid telegraphing if they maintain a slight motion than if they remain perfectly still before attacking.

Enter the contest with an undisturbed mind. Don't worry about winning or losing or try to plan an elaborate strategy in advance. Concentrate on your opponent, seeing his whole body at once. Don't concentrate on any one technique but react as the moment demands. If your attention is drawn to one kick or punch your opponent will make use of your concentration to score with another kick or punch from outside your field of vision. If, on the other hand, you see everything your opponent does, you can make the proper response and execute an effective counter.

Don't repeat the same techniques over and over until they become predictible. Vary your responses and rhythm to confuse your opponent. Make him break rhythm while maintaining your own.

The best defense against an overly aggressive opponent is to retreat until he exposes a weakness, usually during a stance change, and counterattack.

These are basic ideas designed to give the beginner an introduction to the concept of free fighting rather than an exhaustive approach to the subject.

PREARRANGED FIGHTING

Samples of this exercise are performed by prearrangement between attacker and defender. The objective is to teach timing and coordination. Safety must be emphasized.

    1. Attacker and defender face each other and make a bow, approximately 3 feet apart. (1)

    2. Attacker executes a down block while assuming the front stance, (attacker steps backward with either foot), simultaneously the defender makes a ready stance. (*All* prearranged fighting starts with the above two steps.) (2)

Upper Punch and Counter: #1

1. Attacker executes a high punch with right fist at eye level, accompanied by yelling, and advances one step.
2. Defender takes one step backward and executes an upper block, and simultaneously counters with a right high punch to face. (3)

    NOTE: Defender may execute an eye poke or a knife hand chop to temple or neck, accompanied by a yell.

Middle Punch and Counter: #1

1. Attacker executes a middle punch to defender's solar plexus.
2. Defender executes an inside-outside (or outside-inside) middle block after retreating one step, and simultaneously counters with a middle punch to the solar plexus.

    NOTE: Defender may execute a spear hand to solar plexus or an instep kick to the groin.

Low Punch and Counter: #1

1. Attacker executes a low punch aimed at the defender's groin or lower abdomen.
2. Defender takes one step backward while executing a down block, and counters with a down punch to groin. However, he may substitute a high or middle punch. (5)

Upper Punch and Counter: #2

1. Attacker executes an upper or middle punch.
2. Defender drops to one knee and executes a punch to groin. (6)

Middle Punch and Counter: #2

1. Attacker executes a middle punch.
2. Defender steps forward with right foot and assumes a horseback riding stance at right angle to attacker, while executing a middle block. The motion continues with a back fist to bridge of nose. (7) (8)

Why is it important to concentrate on seeing the entire body of your opponent at all times? How do pre-arranged and semi-free fighting differ?

Low Punch and Counter: #2

1. Attacker executes a low punch.
2. Defender takes backward step with right foot, assumes the side horseback riding stance and executes a knife hand down block. (9)
3. Defender pivots to front stance and executes an upper or middle punch. (10)
   NOTE: After pivot to front stance, defender may execute a front kick.

Upper Punch and Counter: #3

1. Attacker executes an upper punch.
2. Defender steps backward, assuming a side stance, parries the punch and carries
   the motion onward to a spear hand or eye poke to face of attacker. (11)
   NOTE: May follow eye poke with a front kick.

Middle Punch and Counter: #3

1. Attacker executes a middle punch.
2. Defender parries punch with a crescent block (kick), and follows with middle
   punch to solar plexus. (12) (13)
   NOTE: After executing the crescent block, the motion may be continued as
   a side kick to the attacker's solar plexus.

Low Punch and Counter: #3

1. Attacker executes a low punch.
2. Defender executes a down block, steps forward and executes a right elbow
   strike to face of attacker. This may be followed by a back fist to the bridge of
   nose. (14) (15)
   NOTE: Defender may secure wrist of attacker prior to the execution of the
   elbow strike.
   SUMMARY: The above one-step techniques may be incorporated into a two-
   or three-step fighting exercise. For example, in three-step fighting: Attacker may
   execute a series of punches. The defender executes the appropriate blocks and
   after the last block, executes a counterattack. Figures shown demonstrate this.
   There are hundreds of combinations of block and counterattacks. This is only
   a small sample.

Example A   Three step pre-arranged fighting.

Example B   Three step pre-arranged fighting.

One step pre-arranged fighting.

1   2   3

4   5   6

7   8   9

10   11   12

13   14   15

ADDITIONAL PREARRANGED FIGHTING

1. The attacker executes a body punch. The defender assumes a front stance and executes an outside-inside body block. He then turns using his lead leg as the point about which he pivots. He then executes an elbow strike to the kidneys. (1) (2)

2. Attacker executes middle punch. Defender steps in, assumes horseback stance and executes an outside-inside body block. Turning the opposite direction, he executes an elbow strike to the solar plexus. (3) (4)

3. Attacker executes a face punch. The defender assumes a back stance and executes a high knife hand block. He pulls the attacker toward him while executing an elbow strike to the chin. (5) (6)

4. Attacker executes a body punch. The defender moves inward into a closed toe attention stance, simultaneously blocking the punch with a knife hand block and executing a knife hand strike to the neck. (7)

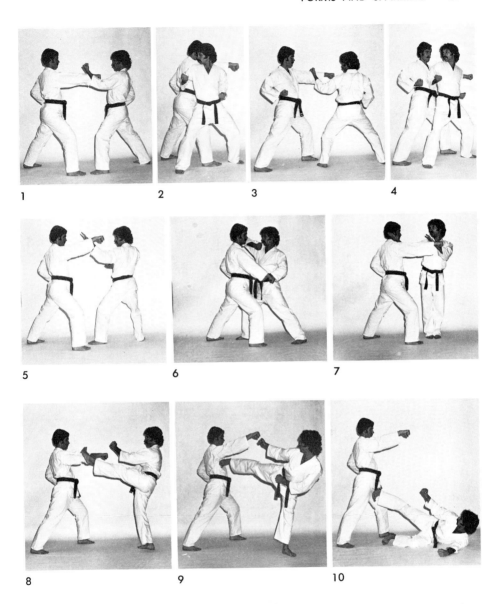

5. Attacker executes a body punch. The defender uses an outside-inside slap kick to deflect the attack. The defender sets his kicking foot down assuming a front stance and counters with a reverse punch. (8)
6. Attacker executes a face punch. The defender sidesteps and executes a side kick to the ribs. Variation—defender executes a sacrifice kick (side thrust kick to the groin). (9) (10)

Language of karate

6

Customarily, throughout the world, the Oriental Martial Arts retain their Oriental language. Japanese or Korean words are spoken by all players and instructors. This custom is not only respectful to the noble heritage of the art but also it is practical since high ranking instructors and visitors naturally use their native language. Although American students are not usually expected to memorize long lists of terms, it is useful to have available a glossary of often used karate words.

TAE KWON DO TERMINOLOGY

Officially and customarily, Korean terms are used in the sport of *Tae Kwon Do* throughout the world. To assist you in pronouncing the Korean words, here are some basic rules of thumb:

The letter "a" is pronounced as the "ah" in father; "o" is sounded like the "o" in "oh"; "i," represents the short sound in "if," and "e," stands for the vowel in "pet"; "ae" is pronounced like the "a" in "May"; "ya" is always the "ya" as in "yacht," but "yu" is the so-called French "u" in "useful," and "wa" is pronounced like the "hwa" sound in "what."

Basic Terms

English	Korean
Ankle	*Bal Mok*
Body	*Mom Tong*
Chin	*Tuk*

English	Korean
Elbow	Pal Gub
Face	Ul Gul
Finger	Sohn Ku Rak
Fist	Ju Mok
Foot	Bal
Front	Ap
Head	Muh Lee
Heel	Bal Deui Geum Chi
Inside	Ahn
Knee	Moo Reub
Left	Wen
Low	A Rae
Neck	Mok
Outside	Ba Got
Posture	Ja Se
Rear	Deui or dwi
Right	Oh Reun
Side	Yop
Waist	Huh Lee
Wrist	Pal Mok

Terms Used in the Training Hall

English	Korean
About-Face	Deui Ro Do Ra
Art of Self-defense	Ho Shin Sul
At Ease	Pyan Yi She-Uh
Attention	Cha Ryo
Reverse	Ban Dae
Basic	Kibon
Basic Movement	Kibon Dong Chak
Begin	Shi Chak
Black Belter	Yu Dan Ja
Bow	Kyung Ye
Breaking	Kyuk Pa
Director (Training hall)	Kwan Jang Nim
End	Geu Man
Instructor	Sa Bom Nim
Movement	Dong Chak
Non Black-Belter	Moo Dan Ja
Sparring	Kyo Reu Gi
Special	Teuk Soo
Special Movement	Teuk Soo Dong Chak

Teacher or Sir	*Sun Sang Nim*
Technique	*Gisul*
Toe	*Bal Ku Rak*
Turn	*Do Ra*
Uniform	*Do Bak*
Vital Points	*Geub So*
Warm-down Exercise	*Chung Lee Un Dong*
Warm-up Exercise	*Joon Bee Un Dong*

Numbers

	For Cadence	For Ranking Order
One	*Ha-na*	*Il*
Two	*Dool*	*Yi*
Three	*Set*	*Sam*
Four	*Net*	*Sa*
Five	*Da-sot*	*Oh*
Six	*Yo-sot*	*Yook*
Seven	*Il Gop*	*Chil*
Eight	*Yo-dol*	*Pal*
Nine	*A-hop*	*Koo*
Ten	*Yol*	*Ship*
Eleven	*Yol Ha-na*	*Ship-Il*
Twenty	*Sumul*	*Yi-Ship*
Twenty-one	*Sumul-Ha-na*	*Yi-Ship-Il*
Thirty	*Sorun*	*Sam Ship*
One Hundred	*Baik*	*Baik*
One Hundred and one	*Baik-Ha-na*	*Baik-il*

Basically, numbers above ten are formed simply by adding the numbers one to nine to the words meaning "ten," "twenty," "thirty," etc. For example, 32=*Sorun-dool*.

Technical Terms

English   **Korean**

FIST: (*Ju Mok*)

1. Backfist   *Deung Ju mok*
2. Fore-fist   *Ju Mok*
3. Hammer-fist (Bottom fist-   *Me Ju mok*
   downward)
4. Middle Finger one-knuckle   *Bam Ju mok*
   fist (Chestnut fist)

English
FIST: (Ju Mok)

5. Open knuckle fist
6. Side-Hammer fist (Bottom fist-sideways)

HAND: (Sohn Nal)

1. Inner Knife Hand
2. Knife Hand
3. One Finger Spear Hand
4. Palm Heel Hand
5. Pliers Hand
6. Rake Hand
7. Scissors Spear Hand
8. Spear Hand
9. Tiger Mouth Hand
10. Two-Finger Spear Hand

FOOT: (Bal)

1. Ball of foot
2. Foot edge
3. Instep

STANCE: (Suh Gi)

1. At-ease Stance
2. Back Stance
3. Crane Stance
4. Crossed-foot Stance (Hooked Stance)
5. Front Stance
6. Forward Pace or Natural Stance
7. Feet Together or Closed-Toe-Stance
8. Horseback Stance
9. Open Toe Stance (Attention Stance)
10. Ready Stance
11. Tiger Stance

KICK: (Cha Gi)

1. Back Kick
2. Crescent Kick

Korean

Pyun Ju mok
Yop Ju mok

Sohn Nal Deung
Sohn Nal
Hahn Sohn Ghoot
Jang Kal
Jip Ke Sohn
Gal Kwi Sohn
Ka We Sohn Ghoot
Sohn Ghoot
Ah Kum Sohn
Doo Sohn Ghoot

Bal Ba Dak
Bal Nal
Bal Deung

Pyun Hee Suh Gi
Deui Koob Yi
Hak Da Lee Suh Gi
Gho Ah Suh Gi

Ap Koob Yi
Ap Suh Gi

Mo Ah Suh Gi

Ju Choom Suh Gi
Cha Ryo Suh Gi

Joon Bee Suh Gi
Bum Suh Gi

Deui Cha Gi
Ban Dal Cha Gi

English	Korean
KICK: (Cha Gi)	
3. Flying Kick	Nop Hee Cha Gi
4. Front Kick	Ap Cha Gi
5. Knee Kick	Moo Reub Cha Gi
6. Round-House Kick	Dol Yo Cha Gi
7. Side Kick	Yop Cha Gi
BLOCK: (Mak Gi)	
1. Augmented Block	Guh Deul A Mak Gi
2. Body Block (Middle Block)	Mom Tong Mak Gi
3. Face Block (Rising Block)	Ul Gul Mak Gi
4. Fist Reverse Wedge Block	Ba Gat Sohn Mok Hea Chuh Mak Gi
5. Knife Hand Block	Sohn Nal Mak Gi
6. Knife Hand Body Block	Sohn Nal Mom Tong Mak Gi
7. Knife Hand Low Block	Sohn Nal A Rae Mak Gi
8. Low Block	A Rae Mak Gi
9. Mountain Block	San Teul Mak Gi
10. Palm Press Block	Ba Tang Sohn Nul Ruh Mak Gi
11. Scissors Block	Ka Wey Mak Gi
12. Side Block	Yop Mak Gi
13. Two Fist Low Block	Aut-Kul-A Mak Gi
14. Two Fist Upper Block	Aut-Kul-A Ul Gul Mak Gi
15. Wedge Block	Hea Chuh Mak Gi
PUNCHES AND STRIKES (Chi Reu Gi & Chee Gi)	
1. Body Punch (Middle Punch)	Mom Tong Chi Reu Gi
2. Body Side Punch	Yop Chi Reu Gi
3. Downward Strike	Nae Ryo Chee Gi
4. Face Punch	Ul Gul Chi Reu Gi
5. Fist-Hammer Blow	Me Ju Mok Chee Gi
6. Knife Hand Strike	Sohn Nal Chee Gi
7. Knife Hand Side Strike	Sohn Nal Ba Gat Chee Gi
8. Low Punch	A Rae Chi Reu Gi
9. Reverse Punch	Ban Dae Chi Reu Gi
10. Uppercut Punch	Je Cho Chi Reu Gi
11. Uppercut Strike	Tuk Chi Reu Gi
12. Vertical Punch	Se Wo Chi Reu Gi

Generally, technical terms are formed by combining words that designate all of the components. For example: face block = Ul Gul + Mak Gi = Ul Gul Mak Gi, and low block = A Rae + Mak Gi = A Rae Mak Gi.

KARATE TERMINOLOGY

The Japanese Terms: The letter "i" is pronounced "ee" as in marine; o is pronounced long as in go; u, as in rule; e as in pen; g, pronounced hard as in goat; ai as in aisle; and ei, as "eh." Thus, some of the terms used in this book are pronounced as follows: Shiai (she-eye), Uke (oo-keh); Karategi (car-ah-tay-gee); sensei (sen-say).

English	Japanese
Art of attacking vital points of the body	Atemi waza
Art of self-defense	Ho shin jitsu
Attention	Kio tsuke
Back (rear)	Uchiro
Back fist	Uraken
Back hand	Hai shu
Back stance	Ko kutsu dachi
Ball of the foot	Chusoku
Begin	Hajime
Belt	Obi
Black belter	Yudansha
Block	Uke
Body area	Chudan
Bow	Re
Cat stance	Neko ashi dachi
Class (ranking)	Kyu
Closed toe stance	Musubi dachi
Contest	Shiai
Combination	Ren raku
Crane stance	Tsuruashi dachi
Dropping	Otoshi
Elbow	Empi or Hiji
Elbow strike	Empi uchi or Hiji ate
Examination	Shinsa
Face	Kao
Face area	Jodan
Fist	Ken
Foot	Soku (ashi)
Foot edge	Sokuto
Form	Kata
Forefinger	Ippon
Front	Mae
Front stance	Zenkutsu dachi
Hammer fist	Kentsui
Hand	Te

English	Japanese
Head	Atama
Heel	Kakato
Hook stance	Kake dachi
Horseback stance (straddle)	Kiba dachi
Instep	Haisoku
Instructor	Sensei
Joint	Kansetsu
Jumping	Tobi
Jump kick	Tobi keri
Kicking	Keri
Knee	Hiza
Knife hand	Shuto
Knife hand block	Shuto uke
Left	Hidari
Lower block	Gedan barai
Lower area of body	Gedan
Lower forearm	Kote
Master instructor	Shihan
Meditation	Zen or mokuso
Navel	Tanden
Non-black belt	Mudansha
Opponent	Aite
Palm Heel	Shotei, Teishi
Player	Senshu
Practice hall	Dojo
Punching board	Maki wara
Ready	Junbi
Rear	Ushiro
Reverse punch	Gyaku
Ridge hand	Haito
Right	Migi
Rooted Stance	Fudo dachi
Roundhouse	Mawashi
Roundhouse kick	Mawashi geri
Side	Yoko
Side kick	Yoko geri
Spear hand	Nukite
Stance	Dachi
Stop	Mate
Strike	Uchi
Swing	Mawashi
Swordsmanship	Kendo
Technique	Waza
Test for breaking power	Tameshi wari

If you are studying TAE KWON DO, can you translate these Korean terms: Sun Sang Nin, Cha Ryo, Shi Chak, Kyung Ye? If you are learning Japanese karate, can you translate these terms: Kio tsuke, Hajime, Re, Sensei?

English	Japanese
Time	Jikan
Triple punch	San ren zuki
Two finger spear	Nihon nukite
Uniform	Gi
U punch	Awase Zu ki
Vital points	Kyu sho
Warrior or samurai	Bushi
Way of the respectable warrior	Bushido
Win by default	Fu sen sho
Wrist	Kokken
X block	Jugi uke
Yell	Kiai

English	Japanese
One	I-chi
Two	Ni
Three	San
Four	Shi
Five	Go
Six	Roku
Seven	Shichi
Eight	Hachi
Nine	Ku
Ten	Ju
Eleven	Ju-ichi
Twenty	Ni-ju
Twenty-one	Ni-ju-I-chi
Thirty	San Ju

Generally numbers above ten are formed by adding the numbers one through nine. For example: 31 = Sanju-ichi in Japanese.

Rules of karate

7

THE CONTEST

One of the ultimate objectives of the art and sport of karate is realized in the free-style sparring of the tournament. The purpose of the tournament is to test skills against unfamiliar opponents. In free-style fighting (Kumite or Dae Ryon) two karate students try, at random, all of their strikes, kicks, blocks and counterattacks. In practice fighting at the weekly classes the sparring is serious and vigorous but the students know each other well and have learned from the same instructor. In the karate tournament (shiai or Shi hap) students from different schools who are strangers to each other are brought together into an eight or nine square yard area and are given the order to begin. The students are paired as to weight and rank but their styles and skills may vary widely. Three minutes later (if a tie there is another bout of two minutes) one of the students will be declared the winner. His style of karate, speed, endurance, fighting spirit, courage, and sportsmanship have been carefully evaluated by five judges all above the rank of 4th degree and sometimes 6th degree black belt. Each free fighting contest symbolizes a life and death struggle and each student, win or lose, knows that that day he or she faced real danger, encountered potential death, and survived the exciting teaching experience.

FROM THE SPECTATOR'S POINT OF VIEW

To the uninitiated spectator watching his or her first karate tournament the contests may seem almost pagan—blood curdling screams, flying kicks aimed at the heart, knife hand chops to the neck—this bare-handed fighting, without armor, looks lethal or at best very dangerous. The novice spectator is amazed that no one is injured, not even a drop of blood drawn. Dozens of contestants enter and leave the square arena not only alive but, more important, embracing like old friends obviously the better for the fighting experience. Most spectators are duly impressed and immediately recognize that karate is a complex art that requires precise, vigorous training. The blows look as if they land at full impact and the blows are powerful; some of the students demonstrate that they can break six pine boards with a single knife hand chop. What is the secret of these "supermen?" The answer, as the reader already knows, is superb training in self-control. The punches do not land at full impact, they are pulled back an inch away from the opponent's body, or sometimes lightly tap the skin not even leaving a bruise. Free fighting is not for the novice white belt. These contestants have been studying basic techniques for months and months. They have perfected control and can hit their target or, more importantly, pull-back their strikes and kicks an inch away from their target.

CONTEST RULES

Contest rules vary only slightly in different tournaments. Time limits may vary from two to seven minutes for each bout (usually three minutes) and this is set before the shiai begins. Four judges and a chief referee are in attendance for each match. In some tournaments, one referee and one judge are used so that more than one contest can occur at the same time. One referee is inside the fight area moving about with the contestants only a foot or so away. Other judges sit at the corners of the contest square. The decision of the five judges is final and irrevocable. The grading is a bit complex. It takes a high ranking karate man to see the fast strikes and accurately determine whether or not the punch would land at a vital point if it were not pulled back. Often the audience is surprised when the winner of a close match is announced. Grading is on a point system, and one point or sometimes two out of three points win the match. Merits and demerits are awarded by the judges. The object is to "hit" with foot or fist a vital point on the opponent's body. The winning punch would be a lethal or "killing point" were the strike delivered at full power and not pulled back. So the contest is quite literally a symbolic dance of instant death. Demerits are given quickly for avoiding fighting or deliberately turning the back to the opponent. Cursing or any unsportsmanlike conduct may bring instant termination of the bout. Any loss of control is verboten. This is a potentially dangerous sport and high ranking judges are close at hand to see that it remains injury free. Fighting spirit and stoicism as well as technique brings merit points but in the final analysis it's all over with one "killing" punch or kick to any one of twenty invisible vital spots on the contestant's body. The matches begin and end with polite karate bows and the rules are strictly obeyed. The referee's commands are simple, "begin," "separate" or "stop." One of the contestants wears a red ribbon looped over his belt and is designated as the red contestant, the other white. Each corner judge carries a red and white flag and signifies the winner of the match by raising one flag. Should an injury occur, an effort is made to determine its cause and the blame may be attached to the victim who rushed into his opponent unwarily. If the attacker is to blame for an injury he loses the contest. In addition to contests between individuals there can also be five-man team contests. In some tournaments, women are allowed to participate in the bouts.

Basically Prohibited Acts in the Tournament

(1) Impolite or abusive language; mean or ungentlemanly conduct and behavior. (2) Uncontrolled attacking of the face with hands, head butting, or elbows. (3) Attacking a partner who has fallen to the floor during the contest. (4) Attacking testicles or the knee joints. (5) Grabbing, tackling, or other dangerous acts. (6) Throwing techniques. (7) Purposefully wasting time during the contest.

In many matches, especially between high ranking black belts, there may be a great deal of slow stalking movements; then, after two minutes of almost no action at all, with eye-blurring speed a foot or fist will lash out and the contest will be over before most of the spectators saw what happened. In lower ranked contests there is usually a great deal of continuous action.

Karate tournaments offer a very exciting day for the spectator and player alike. In addition to actual matches there are usually demonstrations of self-defense techniques, board- and brick-breaking contests, and contests of katas, or forms. Pine boards are broken by fist, knife hand strike, elbow, or kicking techniques. Kata competition often includes women students and the forms are usually performed solo in front of a panel of high ranking judges. All of the karate students as well as the spectators especially enjoy the beautifully intricate forms. Some of the katas or hyongs are fast and powerful; others are like slow motion ballets. The authors warmly invite each reader to watch a local karate tournament the next time one is available.

BASIC RULES OF TAE KWON DO MATCH*

One of the ultimate objectives of the sport and art of Tae Kwon Do is realized in Dae Ryon (free style sparring). Contest rules vary only slightly from one tournament to another. The basic rules of Tae Kwon Do are as follows:
  I. *Officials*
   1. The officials shall include one chief umpire (referee), four deputy umpires and two jurors. (One juror may be used in a small-scale contest.)

*Enacted by the Korea Tae Kwon Do Association on November 3, 1962. Amended four times. Four Amendments on February 5, 1974, excerpted from the official rules which are composed of 14 articles.

Upon what elements of performance are contestants evaluated in Karate and Tae Kwon Do free style sparring? What is a winning punch?

2. Umpire must: hold a Kuk Ki Won-recognized rank of third Dan (black belt) or higher, must have passed a qualifying examination for a referee that was conducted or sanctioned by the Kuk Ki Won, and must have no record of punitive measures taken against him by the Korea Tae Kwon Do Association or any other sports organization.

The chief umpire is chosen from among the senior dans present, and must have a higher rank than the deputy umpires.

3. The chief umpire serves as referee, and declares the beginning and the end of the competition.

The deputy umpires record all warnings immediately, and they mark down the gain and loss of points on the scoring sheet.

The jury must immediately render judgment regarding any error made by the umpires.

II. *Declaration of Warning and Penalty*

The chief umpire (referee) shall warn the contestant immediately when he has committed any of the following acts:

a. holding an opponent's uniform or body
b. tries to avoid sparring and turns his back to his opponent
c. crosses outside the boundary line
d. tries to or succeeds in stalling the contest
e. throws the opponent
f. pretends falsely to be in pain
g. moves around the line
h. attacks the prohibited spots
i. pushes the opponent with shoulder or body; or pushes the opponent with his hands
j. falls down on purpose
k. pushes the opponent down by using the foot
l. attacks the opponent's face with fist

One point shall be declared to the contestant when he incurs the same warning twice in a round.

Deduction of Point

a. attacks the opponent who has fallen on the floor.
b. hurting the face of the opponent with fist.
c. butting or heading against the face or body of the opponent.
d. attacks intentionally after the declaration of "Gal Yo" (break) by the referee.

The order of valid scores shall be determined as follows:

a. a point shall be scored by a single attack with correct posture.

b. attacking the face, flank, abdomen or solar plexus by foot (with the instep, ball of the foot, heel or side edge of the foot) shall be scored.

c. a point shall not be scored if the attack is in sequence as in a "clinching situation" or in very close proximity.

d. a point shall not be scored when a contestant falls down and is in a clinch or is being held directly after the attack.

e. two points shall be scored when the opponent staggers. One point shall be scored when the opponent is hit by the foot on face. One point shall be scored when a fist or foot attack hit on the body. One point shall be scored when the opponent falls down by receiving fist or foot attack even though the contestant was not struck.

The competitors are not allowed to attack the following vital spots of the body:

Front	Rear
Skull	Base of Skull
Bridge of Nose	Base of Neck
Temple	Upper back
Sternum	Kidney
Armpit	Lower back
Knee joints	Tail bone area
Shin	Back of Knee (side of knee)
Instep	Achilles tendon
Groin	

Official rules or technical information can be obtained by writing to the Korea Tae Kwon Do Association, No. 19 Mu Kyo Dong, Chungku Seoul, Korea 100.

National referee certification for Tae Kwon Do information and tournament rules for the Amateur Athletic Union can be obtained by writing to the AAU National Tae Kwon Do Committee in care of Professor Ken Min, Harmon Gymnasium at the University of California at Berkeley, Berkeley, Ca. 94720.

Information on International Referee certification and the World Tae Kwon Do Championships can be obtained by writing to the World Tae Kwon Do Federation (WTF), San 76, Yuk Sam Dong, Sung Dong-ku, Seoul, Korea.

National referee certification for Karate information and tournament rules for the Amateur Athletic Union can be obtained by writing to the AAU National Karate Committee, 3400 West 86th Street, Indianapolis, Indiana 46268. NOTE TO STUDENTS: There are two separate AAU committees for Tae Kwon Do and Karate.

Karate

8

RANKS

Each of the four major styles of karate—Japanese, Korean, Chinese and Okinawan—has its own standards, promotional requirements, and ranking systems. America does not have a karate style of its own; indeed, many Occidental students are exposed to a composite of several of the major styles. At a large tournament one may see a variety of styles, and students from rival schools may wear different colored belts for the same rank.

This mixing of styles and sometimes keen rivalry between the schools leads some beginners to the erroneous conclusion that karate is disorganized. Many of the differences in styles are subtle, there is much overlapping in the techniques of each school, but karate is not disorganized. Complex, yes. Confusing, yes, but not in itself, confused.

Generally, throughout the world, karate ranks in two systems: The Kyu or Gup (class) ranks of nonblack belts (white, yellow, blue or green, and brown or maroon belts) and the Dan (degree) ranks (the ten degrees of black belt, 1st Dan is lowest and 10th Dan is highest). Promotions from one rank to the next, beginning at 10th class white belt, through 1st class brown or maroon belt to 1st black belt on up to 4th or 5th Dan black belt, is awarded by the highest ranking teachers. Rank promotions are determined by demonstrated skills, knowledge about the history, language and personality traits of humility. There is no fixed time between rank promotions since different students will practice different amounts of time in any given week or month. Korean and Japanese students usually practice one to two hours daily, five days per week; whereas American students usually practice one to one and one-half hours two or three times per week. Generally speaking, students who practice five or six hours per week can be promoted through the ten classes of nonblack belts at the rate of a promotion every three or four months. In most schools about 1000 hours of qualified instruction is required before the student is experienced enough to become a 1st Dan black belt. Some Oriental students who commit their entire waking and sleeping life to the daily study of karate can reach the rank of black belt within eighteen months, but two or three years of intense study is the more usual course. Some American students who only practice two or three times per week may well spend six or more years of study before reaching the rank of 1st Dan. Promotion through the Dan ranks is much, much slower and some of the promotions, that is, above the rank of 7th Dan, may require ten or more years in rank; therefore, it is very rare to see an American student above the rank of 5th Dan. Usually a minimum age of seventeen is required for promotion to black belt.

The following are ranking systems for Japanese Karate and Korean Tae Kwon Do:

TABLE 1

Numerical Class	Japanese	Korean	Colors of the Belt	Minimum Time Required
10th Class (lowest) novice	Ju Kyu	Sip Gup (Keub) or Cho Gup	White	Beginning novice
9th Class	Ku Kyu	Koo Gup	White or Orange	3 months
8th Class	Hachi Kyu	Pal Gup	White, Yellow, or Gold	
7th Class	Shichi Kyu	Chil Gup	White, Yellow, or Gold	3 months
6th Class	Rok Kyu	Yook Gup	Green, Blue or Yellow	3 months
5th Class	Go Kyu	Oh Gup	Green, Blue, Yellow	3½ months 3½ months
4th Class	Yon Kyu	Sa Gup	Green, Blue, Yellow, or Brown	
3rd Class	San Kyu	Sam Gup	Brown, Green or Red (maroon)	5-7 months
2nd Class	Ni Kyu	Yi Gup	Brown or Red (maroon)	5-7 months
1st Class	Ik Kyu	Il Gup	Brown or Red Maroon	5-7 months

(highest rank in nonblack belt system and next to first dan black belt)

What qualifications other than demonstration of skill are required for rank promotion? About how many hours of instruction are required to become a 1st Dan Black Belt?

TABLE 2

Dan Rank Numerical	(grade upwards 1st to 10th degree)		Color of the Belt	Minimum Time Required
	Japanese	Korean		
1st Degree (lowest) Dan	Sho-dan Shodan	Cho Dan	Black Belt, Dark Navy Blue	Minimum of 1000 hours under the qualified instructor (since started karate)
2nd Degree Dan	Ni-dan	Yi-dan	Black Belt, Dark Navy Blue	1 year 6 months
3rd Degree Dan	San-dan	Sam-dan	Black Belt, Dark Navy Belt	2 years 6 months
4th Dan	Yo-dan	Sa-dan	Black Belt, Dark Navy Belt	2 years 6 months
5th Dan	Go-dan	Oh-dan	Black Belt, Dark Navy Belt	3 years 6 months
6th Dan	RoKu-dan	Yook Dan	Black Belt, Dark Navy Belt	5 years
7th Dan	Shichi-dan	Chil Dan	Black Belt, Dark Navy Belt	Character, knowledge contribution, personality etc. (7 years)
8th Dan	Hachi dan	Pal Dan	Black Belt, Dark Navy Belt	Same as above (7 yrs-10 years)
9th Dan	Ku dan	Koo Dan	Black Belt, Dark Navy Belt	Same as above (7 yrs-10 years)
10th Dan (highest degree)	Ju dan	Sip Dan	Black Belt, Dark Navy Belt	Same as above 10 years above

PROMOTIONS

Beginning students are naturally quite rank conscious and are often shocked to hear a 1st or 2nd Dan still refer to himself as a beginner, but such is the heritage of the ancient art of karate. No one in a single lifetime can possibly master all there is to know about the art. The more one learns the more one realizes how much more there is to learn. As the new student becomes engrossed in study, he soon loses his rank consciousness and tries to learn all, one lesson at a time. The journey itself should be the goal.

Promotions are achieved by attendance and participation in classes and participation in free fighting at tournaments. A very important factor in promotion is an attitude of humility and good sportsmanship as well as sincere interest in karate. Written and oral examinations are given on details of history and philosophy as well as some basic knowledge about other Oriental Martial Arts. Each student must demonstrate basic skills and the required karate forms to the testor's satisfaction. Some schools conduct examinations for class promotions every three or four months but promotion to the Dan ranks is usually only given in the spring and fall and this promotion usually requires a written thesis and a panel of high ranking judges who officially represent the style or school of karate. All of this rigorous testing guarantees that each legitimately ranked karateka has a well-founded knowledge of his art, can ably control his potentially dangerous skills, and can safely represent karate to others both at home and abroad.

ADVANCED STUDY OF KARATE OR TAE KWON DO

After a basic introduction to the art of karate, after learning the basic skills, lies a complicated network of possible paths to follow. Although the very best karate masters probably still reside in the Orient there are excellent teachers in every major city in the USA and one should do everything possible to locate the best, most qualified instructor. It may be necessary to travel great distances from time to time to check your progress, but it is worth the effort. Books cannot possibly teach by themselves. The teacher, especially for the advanced student, should enter and win competitions, but tournaments alone are not enough. *Black Belt* magazine and *Karate Illustrated* each list dojos across the country. Visit several schools, watch their students in tournaments before deciding on which school to use or ask the advice of the physical education instructor of the local college or Y.M.C.A. if they have a karate program or, if not, who do they recommend.

REQUIREMENTS FOR FIRST-DEGREE BLACK BELT

1. Seventeen years of age (minimum for admission to the senior division).
2. Unquestionably good character and personality.
3. Knowledge and understanding of Tae Kwon Do basics:
   (a) History, philosophy, and principles
   (b) Aims and objectives
   (c) Basic rules
   (d) Safety precautions
   (e) Korean terminology
   (f) Unwritten laws
   (g) Organizations and ranking system
   (h) Sport strategies
   (i) Vital points of the body
4. Proficiency in:
   (a) Fundamentals such as (1) bows, (2) stances, (3) postures, (4) bal-

ance and body deployment, (5) footwork and (6) making a proper Tae Kwon Do fist and executing knife hand skills.

(b) Offensive and defensive techniques: (1) Blocks, (2) Punches, (3) Chops, (4) Pokes, (5) Strikes, (6) Kicks and (7) Methods of avoidance.

(c) Forms: (1) Pal Gye 1-8, and (2) Koryo (nine forms).

(d) Fighting methods: (1) One-step sparring, (2) Two-step sparring, (3) Three-step sparring, (4) Semi-free fighting.

(e) Free-fighting.

(f) Breaking (generally not required).

(g) Practical self-defense techniques.

(h) Service in the development and popularization of Tae Kwon Do.

(i) Assistantship and/or a thesis (if required).

SUGGESTED COURSE CONTENT

The course content can flexibly be divided into twelve to fifteen parts. The following course content is suggested for beginning Tae Kwon Do classes. Once mastered, it will provide the student with numerous skills and basic knowledge.

1. Introduction and orientation
    (a) Class procedure
    (b) Objectives of course
    (c) History and philosophy of Tae Kwon Do
    (d) Lectures on other martial arts and combat sports
    (e) Safety and precautions
    (f) Unwritten laws
    (g) Rules of sport of Tae Kwon Do
    (h) Ranking systems and organizations
    (i) Language of the Tae Kwon Do.
2. Demonstration
    (a) Demonstration of Tae Kwon Do principles and movements.
    (b) Demonstration of offensive and defensive skills.
    (c) Demonstration of forms against imaginary opponents.
    (d) Demonstration of sparring (instructor-assistant).
    (e) Demonstration of power of strikes and kicks.
    (f) Demonstration of practical personal defense.
3. Fundamentals
    (a) Bow
    (b) Stances and balance
    (c) Postures, footwork, body deployment
    (d) Vital points of the body (points that cause injury and pain)
    (e) Learning to make proper fists and knife hands as well as striking surface of the hands, elbows, knees and feet.
    (f) Introduction of warm-up exercises
    (g) Breath control for Tae Kwon Do

4. Introduction to Offensive Skills
   (a) Punches and chops (hands, fists, fingers and elbows)
   (b) Strikes (face, body, low and side)
   (c) Kicking skills (front, side, rear, etc.)
5. Introduction to Defensive Skills
   (a) Blocks
   (b) Methods of avoidance
   (c) Combination blocks
6. Introduction to Poom Se (form practice)-Pal Gye forms
7. Free Activity Week
   (a) Review of all basics
   (b) Formal form practice
   (c) If available, show films or masters' exhibitions
8. Introduction to Applied Practical Self-defense Skills
   (a) Lecture on personal safety tips on the street, at home, in a vehicle, and other places
   (b) Personal defense techniques against physical attack
   (c) Assignments on personal safety tips, crime rate, defense techniques, etc.
9. Introduction to prearranged and semi-prearranged sparrings
   (a) One step sparring
   (b) Two step sparring
   (c) Three step sparring
   (d) Semi-free sparring
10. Mid-term Evaluation
   (a) A skill test (balance, stances, basic skills, Pal Gye forms, one step sparring, and personal defense demonstration)
11. Introduction to the sport of Tae Kwon Do and other Martial Arts
   (a) Tae Kwon Do tournament rules
   (b) Sport strategies
   (c) Safety and tips
   (d) Discussions of other martial arts (judo, aikido, karate, hapkido and others)
   (e) Participation in informal contests
12. Review and Free Activity Week
   (a) Review of all skills which were covered in the class
   (b) Class-required Poom Se practices
   (c) Self-defense techniques
13. Evaluation for Grade
   (a) Skills test for basic skills
   (b) Form demonstration (Poom Se)
   (c) Written test
   (d) Essay for self-defense and safety
14. Evaluation for Tae Kwon Do Belt Rank
   (a) Student demonstration (one, two and three step sparrings)
   (b) Form test
   (c) Self-defense techniques
   (d) Oral examination

Unwritten laws of karate

9

Every sport has its written rules and regulations and every sport also has unwritten customs that are universally practiced. Oriental customs and courtesies often seem strange and quaint, even excessive to the Occidental. Karate's unwritten laws are a very important part of its ancient traditions. Because karate is such a violent and potentially dangerous activity, the discipline and regimentation must be strict in order to control this explosive power. Commands that are questioned rather than followed (then later questioned) could lead to an injury. Forgetting to bow is more than rude, it could be dangerous. Dojo manners are strictly enforced because loud talk and interruptions might distract from important instructions. Concentration is keen and meditation is done in silence. Great respect is accorded the teacher and the senior students. The seniors are committed to teaching their juniors, but the juniors must be humble; this is the noble heritage of karate. In karate, as in the military, rank has its privileges. But rank also has many responsibilities. An important factor in black belt promotions is teaching ability and genuine humility.

GENERAL UNWRITTEN LAWS

1. Karate students are humble and courteous. They do not criticize other styles of karate or other instructors.
2. Karate students must not be boastful and never bullying. Fighting outside of the dojo is never permitted. A karate student may be banned from all further study if he fights or even threatens others, except of course, in a case of life-or-death self-defense.
3. Bowing is the customary greeting of respect to the instructor and to all of the senior teachers both inside and outside of the dojo. Bow upon

entering and leaving the dojo, even in street clothes. Bow when starting and ending a sparring practice and at the start and close of each lesson.

4. Do not interrupt instructions to ask questions—ask politely at the end of class if a question/answer period is not allotted. If tardy to class ask instructor's permission to begin. If leaving the class early get permission first.

5. Silent meditation, standing or kneeling (ZaZen or Ja Sun), should be observed before and after each karate lesson.

6. No smoking, gum chewing or loud talking in the dojo.

7. Never horseplay or roughhouse—karate is deadly serious.

8. In all practice emphasis is placed on control, accuracy, and noncontact.

9. Do not attempt to learn forms or teach them without express permission from the chief instructor.

10. Do not attempt to condition hands, fists, or feet for breaking ability without proper instruction from the teacher.

11. The dojo is to be kept clean by all students. Keep the practice floor dry and pick up objects that might cause injuries. Each student takes his or her turn sweeping the dojo floor.

12. Courtesy and good sportsmanship is a must between all students. In free fighting practice if your opponent makes a particularly good attack and scores a point you should immediately show your respect with a courteous bow before continuing the sparring action.

13. Finally, karate is a strenuous sport and good physical fitness is a necessity. Exercise daily and do good warm-up exercising before lessons and light warm-down exercises at the end of class. Good hygiene is important—keep nails trimmed; keep karate uniform (Gi or Do bok) cleaned; warm showers after each class.

There are many good practice rules to use before, during and after a contest or tournament. These are listed below:

Prior to a Contest

1. No strenuous exercise and no alcoholic beverages for two days prior to a contest.

2. Relax and get plenty of rest. Have a clear mind and a relaxed body.

3. No food during the two hours before the contest. Go to the bathroom before the bout begins.

4. Uniform clean, fingernails and toenails trimmed. If you wear eyeglasses they should be shatterproof.

5. Arrive at the contest area early enough to look around and become familiar with the facilities.

6. Be sure you understand the scoring system, the time limits, and all of the contest rules.

7. Light warm-up exercises then brief meditation just before the contest.

8. Some tension and apprehension is inevitable—your opponent is worried and scared too. Try to relax, be confident.

During the Contest

1. Be ready to move immediately upon the referee's signal. Be prepared both physically and psychologically.
2. Be courteous. Maintain a good spirit—an aggressive attitude.
3. Believe that you will win; self-confidence is most important. Think: "I will—I must."
4. Take initiative—do not try to cover your weakness by constantly retreating. Kiai shouts when you attack and counterattack but no cursing or impolite yelling.
5. Remember, your opponent is getting tired too—hold on, be patient, only a little more time to go—do not give up.
6. Obey the referee and do not protest his decisions.

After the Contest

1. Congratulate your opponent, win or lose.
2. Wipe off sweat and do light warm-down exercises.
3. If you win, be humble; do not boast.
4. If you lose, be a good sport and be gracious. Later, ask the referees and seniors for advice so you can improve in the future.
5. Don't forget to extend thanks to tournament officials. Get acquainted with fellow students and other leading instructors.
6. If time permits participate in the closing ceremonies, in uniform even if you did not win.
7. Try to make each tournament a learning experience. At the end of the day meditate on what you learned.

Conduct of Spectators at a Tournament

1. No sideline coaching.
2. No hats or caps in the tournament halls—keep site clean.
3. Applaud fairly all contestants, especially applaud for fine skill and good sportsmanship.
4. No excessive yelling or even loud talking that might distract from the intense concentration that is required.

In summary, karate's unwritten laws are simply reminders of good manners and should be basic principles in daily life. Karate requires intense concentration. Attentiveness and discipline are prerequisites to safety in the dojo.

Selected references and resources

SELECTED REFERENCES AND RESOURCES

CHO, HENRY SIHAK. *Korean Karate: Free Fighting Techniques.* Rutland, Vt.: Charles E. Tuttle Company, 1968.

CHOI, HONG HI. *Tae Kwon Do: The Art of Self Defense.* Seoul, Korea: Daeha Publishing Company, 1965.

CHUN, RICHARD. *Tae Kwon Do.* New York: Harper & Row, 1976.

COLEMAN, E. and KIM, DAESHIK. "Weight Training for Martial Arts," *Martial Arts Sports.* No. 2, (1976).

FEDERAL BUREAU OF INVESTIGATION. *FBI Uniform Crime Report.* Washington, D. C.: Department of Justice, 1975.

HOOVER, J. E. *Defensive Tactics.* Washington, D. C.: FBI, Department of Justice, 1959.

KIM, DAESHIK and VACALIS, T. D. "Modern Day Women and Self-Defense," *The Progressive Physical Educator,* Phi Delta Pi, Winter, 1969.

KIM, DAESHIK. "Karate: A New Physical Education Activity," *The Physical Educator,* vol. 26, no. 3 (October 1969):115-19.

KIM, DAESHIK, ed. *Tae Kwon Do & Karate Newsletters.* Department of Physical Education, University of Georgia, vol. 1-5, 1969.

――――. *JUDO.* Dubuque, Iowa: Wm. C. Brown Company Publishers, 1977.

――――. "Tae Kwon Do Can Put Spark into Stale P. E. Programs," *Martial Arts Sports.* Chicago: vol. no. 1, 1976.

―――― and RILEY, HUGH. "Self-defense Techniques for Women Under Attack." *Martial Arts Sports.* Chicago: vol. 1, no. 2, 1976.

KIM, UN YONG. *Tae Kwon Do,* the World Tae Kwon Do Federation, 1977.

LAROSE, J. H. and KIM, DAESHIK. "Knuckle Fracture," *Journal of the American Medical Association.* Vol. 21, no. 4, (October 21, 1968): 95-98.

————. "Karate: Hand Conditioning," *Medicine Science in Sports*. American College of Sports Medicine, vol. 1, no. 2, (June 1969): 95-98.

LEE, CHONG W., ed. *Tae Kwon Do Kyo Bon*. Korean Tae Kwon Do Association, 1976.

LELAND, TOM W. "A Psychotherapist and the Oriental Martial Arts," *Voices*. American Academy of Psychotherapists, vol. 1, Winter, 1965.

NAKAYAMA, M. *Dynamic Karate*. New York: Kodansha, 1074.

———— and DRAEGER, D. F. *Practical Karate Series*. Rutland, Vt.: Charles F. Tuttle Company, 1965.

NISHIYAMA, H. and BROWN, R. C. *Karate*. Rutland, Vt.: Charles E. Tuttle Company, 1960.

OYAMA, MASUTATSU. *What is Karate?* Tokyo, Japan: Japan Publications Trading Company, 1966.

————. *This is Karate*. Tokyo, Japan: Japan Publications Company, 1966.

————. *Advanced Karate*. Tokyo, Japan: Japan Publications Company, 1974.

————. *Boy's Karate*. Tokyo, Japan: Japan Publications Company, 1970.

SCHROEDER, CHARLES and WALLACE, BILL. *KARATE*. Reading, Massachusetts: Addison-Wesley Publishing Co., 1976.

SMITH, ROBERT and DRAEGER, D. F. *Asian Fighting Arts*. Palo Alto, Ca.: Kodansha International Ltd., 1969.

SON, DUK SUNG and CLARK, R. J. *Korean Karate: The Art of Tae Kwon Do*. Englewood Cliffs, N. J.: Prentice Hall, Inc., 1968.

MAGAZINES AND OTHERS (Alphabetical Order)

American Tae Kwon Do Newsletter (Ken Min, editor, National AAU Tae Kwon Do Committee)

Black Belt (general monthly publication of the martial arts in the United States)

Karate Illustrated (general monthly publication of karate in the United States)

Martial Arts Sports (general bi-monthly publication of martial arts and sports in the United States)

Modern Karate (general publication of karate. Published by Kyokushinkai-kan in Tokyo, Japan)

Tae Kwon Do (official publication of the Korean Tae Kwon Do Association)

Traditional Tae Kwon Do (general monthly publication of Tae Kwon Do in the United States)

World Tae Kwon Do (official publication of the World Tae Kwon Do Federation)

Appendix: Questions and answers

1. The Oriental bow is *not* given under the following conditions:
   a. before and after contests
   b. in street fighting
   c. upon entering and leaving the dojo
   d. upon greeting the senior instructor in public (p. 15)
2. Combined self defense techniques usually do *not* include which one of the following:
   a. Kendo
   b. Karate
   c. Aikido
   d. Judo (p. 15)
3. Bodhidharma taught meditation and chuan-fa in:
   a. India
   b. Korea
   c. Pakistan
   d. China (p. 1)
4. The ancient forerunner of Korean Tae Kwon Do was:
   a. Kumite
   b. Oyama
   c. Hwang Ki
   d. Tae Kyon (p. 7)
5. Zen Buddhism has been called the religion of:
   a. Hyong
   b. Immediate Reality
   c. Moral Discipline
   d. Soft Tension (p. 12)
6. The headquarters of the World Tae Kwon Do Federation is:
   a. The Kuk Ki Won
   b. The Kodokan
   c. In the United States
   d. In Japan (p. 5)

7. Which of these attacks is prohibited in Karate contests:
   a. attack to knee joints
   b. back kicks to face
   c. kicks to chest and solar plexus
   d. fist to kidney areas (p. 70)
8. In Karate contests, for identification, one contestant usually:
   a. is called Tori
   b. wears black ribbon
   c. wears red ribbon looped through his belt
   d. is called "A" (p. 69)
9. Which of these Katas (forms) are *not* pictured in this book:
   a. Pinan
   b. Naifanchi
   c. Chonji
   d. Koryo (p. 38)
10. Which of these is *not* a basic Karate kick:
    a. side snap kick
    b. eagle kick
    c. front snap kick
    d. round house kick (p. 34)
11. The sport of Judo was founded by:
    a. Mifune
    b. Choi Hong Hi
    c. Mas Oyama
    d. Jigoro Kano (p. 6)
12. Which of these first strikes is a closed hand technique:
    a. Shuto or Soo do
    b. Middle fist punch
    c. spear hand
    d. Palm heel strike (p. 30)
13. Hapkido is:
    a. A combination of karate and jujitsu
    b. Like aikido
    c. An advanced form of judo
    d. None of the above (p. 15)
14. Which of these belt colors are not used by Karate:
    a. black
    b. white
    c. brown
    d. purple (p. 75)
15. The waist twist for additional power is a technique developed by:
    a. Mas Oyama
    b. YMCA Tae Kwon Do Dojang
    c. Okinawan te
    d. Chinese Kempo (p. 11)

COMPLETION

16. "Karate is Zen," so says _____ . (p. 12)
17. Chinese Kempo is thought to be_____ years old. (p. 1)
18. The Karate form is called a_____ in Japanese and_____in Korean. (p. 38)
19. Tai chi chuan means _____. (p. 9)

20. The open hand Karate technique with the fingers up at 90° angle to the arm is called the _____.   (p. 33)
21. Bodhidharma founded the Zen sect at the _____ monastery.   (p. 1)
22. Master Uyeshiba invented the martial art of _____.   (p. 14)
23. In the "attention" stance the toes are open at _____ angle.   (p. 24)
24. Judo contests are won by one point called _____.   (p. 14)
25. The 4 most common stances used in Karate are the _____ stances. (p. 24)
26. The little pea sized pisiform bone of the hand is the weapon area used in the _____ strike.   (p. 22)
27. The Karate yell is called the _____ Japanese or _____ Korean.   (p. 19)
28. The Kata that means "the heaven and the earth" is the _____.   (p. 49)
29. The "Iron hose" Kata is the _____.   (p. 49)
30. The Pal Gye forms are the official forms of the _____.   (p. 38)
31. Free fighting is the _____.   (p. 53)
32. The only way to learn techniques in ancient karate was _____.   (p. 38)
33. Before being introduced to free sparring, the student is taught _____. (p. 53)
34. The martial art that means "the way of spiritual harmony" is _____. (p. 14)
35. In prearranged fighting the attacker after bowing, assumes a _____ block and a _____ stance.   (p. 53)
36. Naifanchi kata is normally introduced at the _____.   (p. 38)
37. Chinese kempo was modified into Okinawa-te as early as _____.   (p. 6)
38. Kung fu styles are broadly divided into _____.   (p. 9)
39. A student's readiness for promotion is determined by _____.   (p. 15)
40. The most important techniques in karate are the _____: (p. 18)
41. The two rearward Karate kicks are the _____ and the _____. (pp. 34-35)
42. The Karate exercise hall is called the _____ Japanese, or _____ Korean. (p. 10)
43. The invisible but very vulnerable points or areas of the body where a strike would cause severe or even lethal damage are called the _____.   (p. 19)
44. Aggression is not merely a response to frustration, it is a deep seated universal _____.   (p. 12)
45. In most Karate movements the center of gravity is _____.   (p. 19)
46. Approximately _____ per cent of the Karate student's time is spent mastering the forms.   (p. 38)
47. The Karate costume is called a _____ Japanese, or _____ Korean.   (p. 16)
48. The Okinawan Karate master who introduced Karate to Japan in 1922 was _____.   (p. 6)
49. The modern Karate master who introduced Karate into the USA in 1952 was _____.   (p. 7)
50. A first degree black belt must have reached a minimum age of _____. (p. 76)

TRUE AND FALSE
51. Kung fu originated in Korea.   (p. 8)
52. Punches to the face are allowed in Tae Kwon Do matches.   (p. 71)
53. Pine boards and even a brick may be broken by the fist, Soo Do Chop, forehead strike and the elbow by some advanced Karatekas.   (p. 70)
54. Kata competitions often include women Karate students.   (p. 70)

55. Cheering and sideline coaching is permitted at Karate Tournaments.   (p. 81)
56. *Black Belt* and *Karate Illustrated* magazines list dojos throughout the country. (p. 76)
57. Karate ranks students in two systems, the Kyu or Gup and the Dan ranks.   (p. 73)
58. Jump kicking is a misnomer, the student does not jump in the air.   (p. 36)
59. The spear hand is used as a block, never a strike.   (p. 30)
60. The side punch is usually delivered from the side stance.   (p. 30)
61. The solar plexus or "Breadbasket" is one of the vital points.   (p. 20)
62. The hands, elbows, knees, feet and forehead are the weapons of the art of Karate. (p. 21)
63. In the Karate fist the 4th and 5th knuckles are the striking surface.   (p. 21)
64. The Okinawans taught "te" in secret for many years.   (p. 6)
65. In Japan today there are as many as 75 different styles of Karate.   (p. 7)
66. Only in recent years has Kumite or free fighting become dangerous.   (p. 7)
67. Hieroglyphics from the Egyptian pyramids showed Karate-like fighting techniques.
                                                                                 (p. 1)
68. The horse-back stance is rarely used by Karate students.   (p. 24)
69. In order to block or strike with maximum power the stance must be perfect.   (p. 24)
70. In the double punch and the U punch both fists are used.   (p. 30)
71. The middle block inside-outside is identical to the outside-inside block.   (p. 2)
72. The elbow strike is performed forward and backward but not sidewards.   (p. 32)
73. The upper and lower X blocks are only used by the fists, not open hand.   (p. 28)
74. Free fighting should be introduced at the white belt level.   (p. 69)
75. The best defense against an overly aggressive opponent is to retreat until he exposes
    an opening and counterattack.   (p. 54)
76. Fighting is never allowed outside the dojo.   (p. 79)
77. The class may be interrupted to ask questions.   (p. 80)
78. In judo the breakfall is the first technique the student learns.   (p. 14)
79. In a contest don't repeat the same techniques so often that you become predictible.
                                                                                 (p. 54)
80. Focus is not important in forms training.   (p. 39)
81. The knife hand face and knife hand body blocks are identical.   (p. 28)
82. Two slaps on the mat is a practice signal for "stop—I surrender."   (p. 14)
83. Karate contests usually have a 3 minute time limit.   (p. 69)
84. Grabbing and tackling is permitted in Karate contests.   (p. 70)
85. The winner in a contest is the one who never needs to counter attack.   (p. 53)
86. Karate students should always be humble and never boastful.   (p. 79)
87. Control and accuracy are less important than speed.   (p. 69)
88. It is O.K. to teach junior students forms without the chief instructor's permission.
                                                                                 (p. 80)
89. 10th Dan is the highest Karate rank.   (p. 75)
90. The maroon belt of Tae Kwon Do is the same rank as the yellow belt of Japanese
    Karate.   (p. 74)
91. In most schools about 1000 hours of instruction is required for promotion to the rank
    of 1st Dan black belt.   (p. 74)
92. Most Karate schools hold promotional examinations every 2 weeks.   (p. 76)
93. There are no Karate teachers above the rank of 3rd Dan in the U.S.A.   (p. 74)
94. The authors of this book are Kim and Leland.   (p. iii)

95. Do not underestimate your opponent. Assume you have one chance. (p. 81)
96. Karate techniques must become automatic. (p. 18)
97. Zen Meditation tries to achieve "no mindedness." (p. 12)
98. Karate is only for the body. (p. 11)
99. Karate is for the mind, body and spirit. (p. 13)
100. Physical readiness is the only prerequisite for promotion. (p. 15)

ANSWERS TO EVALUATION QUESTIONS

Page	Answer and Page Reference
5	No answer
12	No answer
13	Self defense, enjoyment, fitness, mental discipline, inner serenity and responsibility for self and others. (p. viii). No answer for second question.
16	Aikido is a jujitsu-like form of self defense in which the aim is to subdue the opponent without injuring him. (p. 14)
21	Physical control in execution of movements and in stopping short of striking opponent; emotional control in face of danger and in attitudes and behavior toward self and others; intellectual control in mastering the art and meeting the challenges it presents. (pp. 10-13 and others)
24	Horseback, front, back and ready. No answer to second part of question. (p. 24)
31	Low punch—groin; middle punch and double punch—solar plexus; high punch— eye level; side punch—point level with own shoulder; U punch—eye level and groin. (p. 30)
37	Side snap kick, side thrust, round house kick, side jump kick, flying round house kick, and flying side kick (pp. 30-37)
40	A combination of blocks, kicks, and strikes in order to defend against attack from several different directions. There are more than 100 forms. About 10 are required for Black Belt rank, and probably no more than 12 will be mastered in a lifetime of study. (p. 38)
56	If you focus on one movement, opponent will try to kick or punch from outside your field of vision. In prearranged fighting, all moves of attacker and defender are planned in advance. In semi-free fighting, a planned series of moves may be executed in any sequence desired. (pp. 53, 55)
67	Korean terms: teacher, attention, begin and bow. Japanese terms: attention, begin, bow, and instructor. (pp. 61-62, 65-66)
71	Style, speed, endurance, fighting spirit, courage, and sportsmanship. A winning punch is one that would have been lethal had it struck. (pp. 68, 69)
75	Knowledge of history and language and attitude of humility. About 1,000 hours of instruction. (pp. 73-74)

QUESTION ANSWER KEY

Multiple Choice

1. b	4. d	7. a	10. b	13. a
2. a	5. b	8. c	11. d	14. d
3. d	6. a	9. a	12. b	15. b

Completion

16. Mas Oyama
17. 5000
18. Kata; Hyong
19. grand terminus pugilism
20. palm heel strike
21. Shaolin-ssu
22. Aikido
23. 45°
24. ippon
25. front, side, back and horse back
26. Shuto or Soo do
27. Kiai; Kihap
28. Chonji
29. Naifanchi
30. World Tae Kwon Do Federation
31. simulation of combat
32. form practice
33. prearranged fighting

34. Aikido
35. down; front
36. brown belt level
37. 1100 A.D.
38. external and internal
39. good character and technical ability
40. basic skills
41. back kick; back swing kick
42. Dojo; Dojang
43. vital points
44. drive
45. low
46. 40
47. Gi; DoBok
48. G. Funakoshi
49. Mas Oyama
50. seventeen

True and False

51. T	61. T	71. F	81. T	91. T
52. T	62. T	72. F	82. T	92. F
53. T	63. F	73. F	83. T	93. F
54. T	64. T	74. F	84. F	94. T
55. F	65. T	75. T	85. F	95. T
56. T	66. F	76. T	86. T	96. T
57. T	67. T	77. T	87. F	97. T
58. F	68. F	78. T	88. F	98. F
59. F	69. T	79. T	89. T	99. T
60. T	70. T	80. T	90. F	100. F

Index